P9-CQZ-316

# TRUE TO THE FAITH

## A GOSPEL REFERENCE

Published by
The Church of Jesus Christ of Latter-day Saints
Salt Lake City, Utah

# MESSAGE FROM THE FIRST PRESIDENCY

This book is designed as a companion to your study of the scriptures and the teachings of latter-day prophets. We encourage you to refer to it as you study and apply gospel principles. Use it as a resource when you prepare talks, teach classes, and answer questions about the Church.

As you learn gospel truths, you will increase in your understanding of Heavenly Father's eternal plan. With this understanding as a foundation for your life, you will be able to make wise choices, live in harmony with God's will, and find joy in living. Your testimony will grow stronger. You will remain true to the faith.

We are especially mindful of youth, young single adults, and new converts. We promise you that through regular personal prayer and study of the scriptures and the doctrines of the gospel you will be prepared to withstand evil influences that would deceive you and harm you.

May this book strengthen you in your efforts to draw near to the Savior and follow His example.

The First Presidency

# GOSPEL TOPICS
## ARRANGED ALPHABETICALLY

## Aaronic Priesthood

As the Prophet Joseph Smith translated the Book of Mormon, he found mention of baptism for the remission of sins. On May 15, 1829, he and his scribe Oliver Cowdery went into the woods to inquire of the Lord concerning baptism. As they prayed, "a messenger from heaven descended in a cloud of light." This messenger was John the Baptist, the prophet who had baptized Jesus Christ centuries earlier. John the Baptist, now a resurrected being, laid his hands on Joseph and on Oliver and conferred upon each of them the Aaronic Priesthood, which had been taken from the earth during the Great Apostasy. With this authority, Joseph and Oliver were able to baptize one another. (See Joseph Smith—History 1:68–72.)

In the Church today, worthy male members may receive the Aaronic Priesthood beginning at age 12. They receive many opportunities to participate in sacred priesthood ordinances and give service. As they worthily fulfill their duties, they act in the name of the Lord to help others receive the blessings of the gospel.

The offices of the Aaronic Priesthood are bishop, priest, teacher, and deacon. With the authorization of the presiding priesthood leader (usually the bishop or branch president), deacons pass the sacrament. They help the bishop or branch president watch over Church members by giving service and assisting with temporal matters such as gathering fast offerings. Teachers may perform all the duties of deacons, and they also receive other opportunities to serve. They prepare the sacramental bread and water and serve as home teachers. Priests may perform all the duties of deacons and teachers. With the authorization of the presiding priesthood leader, they may also bless the sacrament, baptize, and ordain others to the offices of priest, teacher, and deacon.

The Aaronic Priesthood is "an appendage to the greater, or the Melchizedek Priesthood" (D&C 107:14). It is often called the preparatory priesthood. As a priesthood holder serves in the Aaronic Priesthood, he prepares to receive the Melchizedek Priesthood, to receive the blessings of the temple, to serve a full-time mission, to be a loving husband and father, and to continue in lifelong service to the Lord.

*See also* Melchizedek Priesthood; Priesthood

## Abortion

In today's society, abortion has become a common practice, defended by deceptive arguments. If you face questions about this matter, you can be secure in following the revealed will of the Lord. Latter-day prophets have denounced abortion, referring to the Lord's declaration, "Thou shalt not . . . kill, nor do anything like unto it" (D&C 59:6). Their counsel on the matter is clear: Members of The Church of Jesus Christ of Latter-day Saints must not submit to, perform, encourage, pay for, or arrange for an abortion. If you encourage an abortion in any way, you may be subject to Church discipline.

Church leaders have said that some exceptional circumstances may justify an abortion, such as when pregnancy is the result of incest or rape, when the life or health of the mother is judged by competent medical authority to be in serious jeopardy, or when the fetus is known by competent medical authority to have severe defects that will not allow the baby to survive beyond birth. But even these circumstances do not automatically justify an abortion. Those who face such circumstances should consider abortion only after consulting with their local Church leaders and receiving a confirmation through earnest prayer.

When a child is conceived out of wedlock, the best option is for the mother and father of the child to marry and work toward establishing an eternal family relationship. If a successful marriage is unlikely, they should place the child for adoption, preferably through LDS Family Services (see "Adoption," pages 7–8).

## Abrahamic Covenant

Abraham received the gospel and was ordained a high priest (see D&C 84:14; Abraham 1:2). He later entered into celestial marriage, which is the covenant of exaltation (see D&C 131:1–4; 132:19, 29). In connection with the covenants he made, he received great promises from the Lord concerning his family. Among these promises were the following:

- His posterity would be numerous (see Genesis 17:5–6; Abraham 2:9; 3:14).
- His seed, or descendants, would receive the gospel and bear the priesthood (see Abraham 2:9).
- Through the ministry of his seed, "all the families of the earth [would] be blessed, even with the blessings of the Gospel, which are the blessings of salvation, even of life eternal" (Abraham 2:11).

Together, all the covenants and promises that Abraham received from the Lord are called the Abrahamic covenant. It is an everlasting covenant that extends to all of Abraham's seed (see Genesis 17:7). To be counted as Abraham's seed, an individual must obey the laws and ordinances of the gospel. Then that person can receive all the blessings of the Abrahamic covenant, even if he or she is not a literal descendant of Abraham (see Galatians 3:26–29; 4:1–7; D&C 84:33–40).

As a member of The Church of Jesus Christ of Latter-day Saints, you are a child of the covenant (see 3 Nephi 20:25–26). You have received the everlasting gospel and inherited the same promises given to Abraham, Isaac, and Jacob. You have the right to the blessings of the priesthood and to eternal life, according to your faithfulness in receiving the ordinances of salvation and keeping the associated covenants. Nations of the earth will be blessed by your efforts and by the labors of your posterity.

*See also* Covenant; Eternal Life; Ordinances; Patriarchal Blessings; Priesthood

## Abuse

Abuse is the treatment of others or self in a way that causes injury or offense. It harms the mind and the spirit and often injures the body as well. It can cause confusion, doubt, mistrust, and fear. It is a violation of the laws of society and is in total opposition to the teachings of the Savior. The Lord condemns abusive behavior in any form—physical, sexual, verbal, or emotional. Abusive behavior may lead to Church discipline.

Counsel for the Abuser

If you have been abusive in any relationship, you must repent of your sin. Plead with the Lord to forgive you. Ask for forgiveness from those you have harmed. Speak with your bishop or branch president so he can help you through the repentance process and, if necessary, help you receive additional counseling or other assistance.

If feelings of anger have fueled your abusive behavior, learn to master your temper. Go to the Lord in prayer and ask Him to help you. With an eternal perspective, you will see that your anger has almost always come in response to things that are not very important.

If you have been guilty of sexual abuse, seek to discipline your mind. Remember that your thoughts have a powerful impact on your life—"as [a man] thinketh in his heart, so is he" (Proverbs 23:7). Stay away from pornography and anything else that could stimulate immoral sexual desire. Pray for the ability to "let virtue garnish thy thoughts unceasingly" (D&C 121:45).

Help for Victims of Abuse

If you are a victim of abuse, seek help immediately. Talk with your priesthood leader, normally your bishop or branch president but at times a member of the stake or district presidency. He can help you know what to do.

Be assured that you are not to blame for the harmful behavior of others. You do not need to feel guilt. If you have been a victim of rape or other sexual abuse, whether you have been abused by an acquaintance, a stranger, or even a family member, you are not guilty of sexual sin. Know that you are innocent and that your Heavenly Father loves you.

Pray for the peace that comes only through Jesus Christ and His Atonement (see John 14:27; 16:33). The Savior has experienced all your pains and afflictions, even those caused by others, and He knows how to help you (see Alma 7:11–12). Rather than seek revenge, focus on matters you can control, such as your own outlook on life. Pray for the strength to forgive those who have hurt you.

Continue to seek help from your priesthood leader so he can guide you through the process of emotional healing. Through the blessings of the gospel, you can stop the cycle of abuse and be freed from the suffering you have experienced.

Additional references: Matthew 18:1–6; D&C 121:34–46

*See also* Forgiveness; Repentance

**Addiction** (*See* Gambling; Pornography; Word of Wisdom)

## Adoption

Children are entitled to be raised by parents who honor marital vows and who provide love and support. Adoption can be a great blessing for many children who are born without this opportunity.

When a child is conceived out of wedlock, the best option is for the mother and father of the child to marry and work toward establishing an eternal family relationship. If a successful marriage is unlikely, they should place the child for adoption, preferably through LDS Family Services. Placing the infant for adoption through LDS Family Services helps unwed parents do what is best for the child. It ensures that the child will be sealed to a mother and a father in the temple, and it enhances the prospect for the blessings of the gospel in the lives of all concerned. Adoption is an unselfish, loving decision that blesses the birth parents, the child, and the adoptive family.

If you are married and you and your spouse want to adopt a child, be sure you know all legal requirements of the countries and governmental agencies that are involved. Counsel with your priesthood leaders and, if possible, with staff members in LDS Family Services. If LDS Family Services is not available in your area, work with your priesthood leaders to locate licensed, authorized agencies that protect both the children and the adoptive parents.

## Adultery (*See* Chastity)

## Adversity

As part of Heavenly Father's plan of redemption, you experience adversity during mortality. Trials, disappointments, sadness, sickness, and heartache are a difficult part of life, but they can lead to spiritual growth, refinement, and progress as you turn to the Lord.

Adversity comes from different sources. You may at times face trials as a consequence of your own pride and disobedience. These trials can be avoided through righteous living. Other trials are simply a natural part of life and may come at times when you are living righteously. For example, you may experience trials in times of sickness or uncertainty or at the deaths of loved ones. Adversity may sometimes come because of others' poor choices and hurtful words and actions.

Responding to Adversity with Faith

Your success and happiness, both now and in the eternities, depend largely on your responses to the difficulties of life.

An account in the Book of Mormon illustrates different responses to adversity. The prophet Lehi and his family had been traveling in the wilderness for several days, using their bows and arrows to hunt for food. The family encountered difficulties when Lehi's sons lost the use of their bows. Laman and Lemuel's bows lost their spring, and Nephi's broke. Hungry and tired, Laman and Lemuel began to complain against the Lord. Even Lehi began to murmur. Nephi, on the other hand, refused to be discouraged. He went to work. He recounted: "I, Nephi, did make out of wood a bow, and out of a straight stick, an arrow; wherefore, I did arm myself with a bow and an arrow, with a sling and with stones. And I said unto my father: Whither shall I go to obtain food?" Humbled because of Nephi's words, Lehi asked the Lord where they should go for food. The Lord answered his prayers and led Nephi to a place where he could obtain food. (See 1 Nephi 16:15–31.)

When some people face adversity, they are like Laman and Lemuel. They complain and become bitter. They ask questions like "Why does this have to happen to me? Why do I have to suffer this now? What have I done to deserve this?" But these questions have the power to dominate their thoughts. Such questions can overtake their vision, absorb their energy, and deprive them of the experiences the Lord wants them to receive. Rather than responding in this way, you should follow Nephi's example. Consider asking questions such as, "What am I to do? What am I to learn from this experience? What am I to change? Whom am I to help? How can I remember my many blessings in times of trial?"

Different kinds of adversity require different responses. For example, if you are stricken with illness, you may simply need to be patient and faithful. If you suffer because of others' words or actions, you should work toward forgiving those who have offended you. If you are a victim of abuse, you should seek help immediately. If trials come because of your own disobedience, you should correct your behavior and humbly seek forgiveness.

Although some of your responses to adversity will vary, one response should be constant—your trust in Heavenly Father and Jesus Christ. The prophet Alma taught, "Whosoever shall put their trust in God shall be supported in their trials, and their troubles, and their afflictions, and shall be lifted up at the last day" (Alma 36:3).

## Trusting in Heavenly Father and Jesus Christ

When you trust in the Father and the Son, you are confident that They love you perfectly—that They want you to be happy and that They will help you grow spiritually. You keep the commandments. You seek to know Their will, and you do what They require even when you desire something else. Your prayers for relief are accompanied by the understanding that Heavenly Father will not resolve all matters immediately—that He may allow you to wait so you can continue to learn and grow. Through it all, you find comfort in the assurance that the Savior understands your trials perfectly. As part of His infinite Atonement, He took upon Himself "the pains and the sicknesses of his people." He took upon Himself "their infirmities, that his bowels may be filled with mercy, according to the flesh, that he may know according to the flesh how to succor his people according to their infirmities" (Alma 7:11–12). Because He has experienced your pain, He knows how to help you. If you look to Him in faith, He will strengthen you to withstand any trial you experience.

As you strive to trust the Lord during times of trial, remember the following counsel given through the Prophet Joseph Smith:

"He that is faithful in tribulation, the reward of the same is greater in the kingdom of heaven.

"Ye cannot behold with your natural eyes, for the present time, the design of your God concerning those things which shall come hereafter, and the glory which shall follow after much tribulation.

"For after much tribulation come the blessings" (D&C 58:2–4).

Finding Peace and Joy during Adversity

You can find peace and joy even when you wrestle with challenges and sadness. The Book of Mormon includes an account of a righteous people who learned this truth. Suffering in bondage under a cruel ruler, they poured out their hearts to God (see Mosiah 24:8–12). The Lord answered:

"Lift up your heads and be of good comfort, for I know of the covenant which ye have made unto me; and I will covenant with my people and deliver them out of bondage.

"And I will also ease the burdens which are put upon your shoulders, that even you cannot feel them upon your backs, even while you are in bondage; and this will I do that ye may stand as witnesses for me hereafter, and that ye may know of a surety that I, the Lord God, do visit my people in their afflictions" (Mosiah 24:13–14).

The people responded with faith, and "the burdens which were laid upon [them] were made light; yea, the Lord did strengthen them that they could bear up their burdens with ease, and they did submit cheerfully and with patience to all the will of the Lord" (Mosiah 24:15).

Like these righteous people, you can "submit cheerfully and with patience to all the will of the Lord," knowing that He will strengthen you in your trials. He has promised, "All things wherewith you have been afflicted shall work together for your good, and to my name's glory" (D&C 98:3).

Additional references: Hebrews 4:15–16; 2 Nephi 2:11–24; Mosiah 23:21–22; D&C 105:6; 121:7–9; 122

*See also* Forgiveness; Hope; Peace; Plan of Salvation; Repentance

## Agency

Your Heavenly Father has given you agency, the ability to choose and to act for yourself. Agency is essential in the plan of salvation. Without it, you would not be able to learn or progress or follow the Savior. With it, you are "free to choose liberty and eternal life, through the great Mediator of all men, or to choose captivity and death, according to the captivity and power of the devil" (2 Nephi 2:27).

You had the power to choose even before you were born. In the premortal Council in Heaven, Heavenly Father presented His plan, which included the principle of agency. Lucifer rebelled and "sought to destroy the agency of man" (Moses 4:3). As a result, Lucifer and all those who followed him were denied the privilege of receiving a mortal body. Your presence on the earth confirms that you exercised your agency to follow Heavenly Father's plan.

In mortality, you continue to have agency. Your use of this gift determines your happiness or misery in this life and in the life to come. You are free to choose and act, but you are not free to choose the consequences of your actions. The consequences may not be immediate, but they will always follow. Choices of good and righteousness lead to happiness, peace, and eternal life, while choices of sin and evil eventually lead to heartache and misery.

You are responsible for the decisions you make. You should not blame your circumstances, your family, or your friends if you choose to disobey God's commandments. You are a child of God with great strength. You have the ability to choose righteousness and happiness, regardless of your circumstances.

You are also responsible for developing the abilities and talents Heavenly Father has given you. You are accountable to Him for what you do with your abilities and how you use your time. Do not idle away your time. Be willing to work hard. Choose to do many good things of your own free will.

Additional references: Deuteronomy 11:26–28; 30:15–20; Joshua 24:14–15; 2 Nephi 2; Helaman 14:30–31; D&C 58:26–28; 101:78

*See also* Obedience; Plan of Salvation; Temptation

**Alcohol** (*See* Word of Wisdom)

## Apostasy

When individuals or groups of people turn away from the principles of the gospel, they are in a state of apostasy.

Periods of general apostasy have occurred throughout the history of the world. After times of righteousness, people have often turned to wickedness. One example is the Great Apostasy, which occurred after the Savior established His Church. After the deaths of the Savior and His Apostles, men corrupted the principles of the gospel and made unauthorized changes in Church organization and priesthood ordinances. Because of this widespread wickedness, the Lord withdrew the authority of the priesthood from the earth.

During the Great Apostasy, people were without divine direction from living prophets. Many churches were established, but they did not have priesthood power to lead people to the true knowledge of God the Father and Jesus Christ. Parts of the holy scriptures were corrupted or lost, and no one had the authority to confer the gift of the Holy Ghost or perform other priesthood ordinances. This apostasy lasted until Heavenly Father and His Beloved Son appeared to Joseph Smith in 1820 and initiated the restoration of the fulness of the gospel.

We now live in a time when the gospel of Jesus Christ has been restored. But unlike the Church in times past, The Church of Jesus Christ of Latter-day Saints will not be overcome by general apostasy. The scriptures teach that the Church will never again be destroyed (see D&C 138:44; see also Daniel 2:44).

Although there will not be another general apostasy from the truth, we must each guard against personal apostasy. You can safeguard yourself against personal apostasy by keeping your covenants, obeying the commandments, following Church leaders, partaking of the sacrament, and constantly strengthening your testimony through daily scripture study, prayer, and service.

Additional references: Isaiah 24:5; Amos 8:11–12; Matthew 24:4–14; Acts 20:28–30; 2 Timothy 3:1–5, 14–15; 4:3–4; 1 Nephi 13:24–29; Mormon 1:13–14; D&C 1:15–17; Joseph Smith—History 1:17–19

*See also* Church Administration; Priesthood; Restoration of the Gospel

**Apostle** (*See* Church Administration; Prophets)

**Area Authority Seventy** (*See* Church Administration)

## Articles of Faith

The Articles of Faith outline 13 basic points of belief among members of The Church of Jesus Christ of Latter-day Saints. The Prophet Joseph Smith first wrote them in a letter to John Wentworth, a newspaper editor, in response to Mr. Wentworth's request to know what members of the Church believed. They were subsequently published in Church periodicals. They are now regarded as scripture and included in the Pearl of Great Price.

## Atonement of Jesus Christ

The word *atone* means to reconcile, or to restore to harmony. Through the Atonement of Jesus Christ, we can be reconciled to our Heavenly Father (see Romans 5:10–11; 2 Nephi 25:23; Jacob 4:11). We can ultimately dwell in His presence forever, having been "made perfect through Jesus" (see D&C 76:62, 69).

Jesus Christ "was prepared from the foundation of the world to redeem [His] people" (Ether 3:14). In the premortal spirit world, Heavenly Father presented the eternal plan of salvation, which required an infinite and eternal Atonement. The premortal Jesus, then known as Jehovah, humbly declared that He would do the will of the Father in fulfilling the plan (see Moses 4:2). Thus He was foreordained to carry out the Atonement—to come to the earth, suffer the penalty for our sins, die on the cross, and be resurrected. He became "the Lamb slain from the foundation of the world" (Revelation 13:8; see also 1 Peter 1:19–20; Moses 7:47).

The Atonement is the supreme expression of our Heavenly Father's love for us (see John 3:16). It is also the greatest expression of the Savior's love for the Father and for us (see John 14:28–31; 15:9–13; 1 John 3:16; D&C 34:3; 138:1–4).

Our Need for the Atonement

As descendants of Adam and Eve, all people inherit the effects of the Fall. We all experience spiritual death, being separated from the presence of God, and we are all subject to temporal death, which is the death of the physical body (see Alma 42:6–9; D&C 29:41–42).

In our fallen state, we are subject to opposition and temptation. When we give in to temptation, we distance ourselves from God and come short of His glory (see Romans 3:23).

Eternal justice demands that the effects of the Fall remain and that we be punished for our own wrongdoings. Without the Atonement, spiritual and temporal death would place an impassable barrier between us and God. Because we cannot save ourselves from the Fall or from our own sins, we would be forever separated from our Heavenly Father, for "no unclean thing can dwell . . . in his presence" (Moses 6:57).

The only way for us to be saved is for someone else to rescue us. We need someone who can satisfy the demands of justice—standing in our place to assume the burden of the Fall and to pay the price for our sins. Jesus Christ has always been the only one capable of making such a sacrifice.

## Jesus Christ, Our Only Hope

From before the Creation of the earth, the Savior has been our only hope for "peace in this world, and eternal life in the world to come" (D&C 59:23).

Only He had the power to lay down His life and take it up again. From His mortal mother, Mary, He inherited the ability to die. From His immortal Father, He inherited the power to overcome death. He declared, "As the Father hath life in himself; so hath he given to the Son to have life in himself" (John 5:26).

Only He could redeem us from our sins. God the Father gave Him this power (see Helaman 5:11). The Savior was able to receive this power and carry out the Atonement because He kept Himself free from sin: "He suffered temptations but gave no heed unto them" (D&C 20:22). Having lived a perfect, sinless life, He was free from the demands of justice. Because He had the power of redemption and because He had no debt to justice, he could pay the debt for those who repent. He can say:

"Father, behold the sufferings and death of him who did no sin, in whom thou wast well pleased; behold the blood of thy Son which was shed, the blood of him whom thou gavest that thyself might be glorified;

"Wherefore, Father, spare these my brethren that believe on my name, that they may come unto me and have everlasting life" (D&C 45:4–5).

Truly, "there shall be no other name given nor any other way nor means whereby salvation can come unto the children of men, only in and through the name of Christ, the Lord Omnipotent" (Mosiah 3:17).

The Atoning Sacrifice

Jesus's atoning sacrifice took place in the Garden of Gethsemane and on the cross at Calvary. In Gethsemane He submitted to the will of the Father and began to take upon Himself the sins of all people. He has revealed some of what He experienced as He paid the price for our sins:

"I, God, have suffered these things for all, that they might not suffer if they would repent;

"But if they would not repent they must suffer even as I;

"Which suffering caused myself, even God, the greatest of all, to tremble because of pain, and to bleed at every pore, and to suffer both body and spirit—and would that I might not drink the bitter cup, and shrink—

"Nevertheless, glory be to the Father, and I partook and finished my preparations unto the children of men" (D&C 19:16–19; see also Luke 22:44; Mosiah 3:7).

The Savior continued to suffer for our sins when He allowed Himself to be crucified—"lifted up upon the cross and slain for the sins of the world" (1 Nephi 11:33).

On the cross, He allowed Himself to die. His body was then laid in a tomb until He was resurrected and became "the firstfruits of them that slept" (1 Corinthians 15:20). Through His death and Resurrection, He overcame physical death for us all. He later said:

"I came into the world to do the will of my Father, because my Father sent me.

"And my Father sent me that I might be lifted up upon the cross; and after that I had been lifted up upon the cross, that I might draw all men unto me, that as I have been lifted up by men even so should men be lifted up by the Father, to stand before me, to be judged of their works, whether they be good or whether they be evil—

"And for this cause have I been lifted up; therefore, according to the power of the Father I will draw all men unto me, that they may be judged according to their works.

"And it shall come to pass, that whoso repenteth and is baptized in my name shall be filled; and if he endureth to the end, behold, him will I hold guiltless before my Father at that day when I shall stand to judge the world" (3 Nephi 27:13–16).

## Universal Redemption from the Fall

Through the Atonement, Jesus Christ redeems all people from the effects of the Fall. All people who have ever lived on the earth and who ever will live on the earth will be resurrected and brought back into the presence of God to be judged (see 2 Nephi 2:5–10; Helaman 14:15–17). Through the Savior's gift of mercy and redeeming grace, we will all receive the gift of immortality and live forever in glorified, resurrected bodies.

## Salvation from Our Sins

Although we are redeemed unconditionally from the universal effects of the Fall, we are accountable for our own sins. But we can be forgiven and cleansed from the stain of sin if we "apply the atoning blood of Christ" (Mosiah 4:2). We must exercise faith in Jesus Christ, repent, be baptized for the remission of sins, and receive the gift of the Holy Ghost. Alma counseled:

"Ye must repent, and be born again; for the Spirit saith if ye are not born again ye cannot inherit the kingdom of heaven; therefore come and be baptized unto repentance, that ye may be washed from your sins, that ye may have faith on the Lamb of God, who taketh away the sins of the world, who is mighty to save and to cleanse from all unrighteousness" (Alma 7:14).

## The Gift of Eternal Life

The Savior has declared that eternal life is "the greatest of all the gifts of God" (D&C 14:7). To gain eternal life is to be made worthy to dwell in God's presence, inheriting a place in the highest degree of the celestial kingdom. This gift is available only through the Atonement of Jesus Christ. Mormon said: "What is it that ye shall hope for? Behold I say unto you that ye shall have hope through the atonement of Christ and the power of his resurrection, to be raised unto life eternal, and this because of your faith in him according to the promise" (Moroni 7:41).

To receive this gift, we must meet certain conditions. We must exercise faith in Jesus Christ, repent of our sins, and endure faithfully to the end. We must receive the ordinances of salvation: baptism, the gift of the Holy Ghost, Melchizedek Priesthood ordination (for men), and the temple endowment and marriage sealing. By receiving these ordinances and keeping the associated covenants, we come unto Christ and ultimately receive the gift of eternal life (see Articles of Faith 1:3).

In His infinite justice and mercy, the Lord also gives eternal life to "all who have died without a knowledge of this gospel, who would have received it if they had been permitted to tarry" and to "all children who die before they arrive at the years of accountability" (D&C 137:7, 10).

The Savior invites us all to receive eternal life: "He sendeth an invitation unto all men, for the arms of mercy are extended towards them, and he saith: Repent, and I will receive you. Yea, he saith: Come unto me and ye shall partake of the fruit of the tree of life; yea, ye shall eat and drink of the bread and the waters of life freely" (Alma 5:33–34).

## Finding Peace and Healing through the Atonement

The blessings of the Savior's Atonement extend throughout eternity, but they also come in this life. As you come unto Christ, you will know the joy of being clean before the Lord. You will be able to echo the words of Alma, who, after much sin and rebellion, experienced the painful but healing process of repentance. After he had been forgiven, he testified:

"I could remember my pains no more; yea, I was harrowed up by the memory of my sins no more.

"And oh, what joy, and what marvelous light I did behold; yea, my soul was filled with joy as exceeding as was my pain!

". . . There could be nothing so exquisite and so bitter as were my pains. . . . On the other hand, there can be nothing so exquisite and sweet as was my joy" (Alma 36:19–21).

In addition to offering redemption from the pain of sin, the Savior offers peace in times of trial. As part of His Atonement, Jesus took upon Himself the pains, sicknesses, and infirmities of all people (see Alma 7:11–12). He understands your suffering because He has experienced it. With this perfect understanding, He knows how to help you. You can cast "all your care upon him; for he careth for you" (1 Peter 5:7).

Through your faith and righteousness and through His atoning sacrifice, all the inequities, injuries, and pains of this life can be fully compensated for and made right. Blessings denied in this life will be given in the eternities. And although He may not relieve all your suffering now, He will bless you with comfort and understanding and with strength to "bear up [your] burdens with ease" (Mosiah 24:15).

"Come unto me, all ye that labour and are heavy laden," the Savior said, "and I will give you rest" (Matthew 11:28). On another occasion He again promised His peace, saying, "In the world ye shall have tribulation: but be of good cheer; I have overcome the world" (John 16:33). These are the promises of the Atonement, in this life and throughout eternity.

Additional references: Isaiah 49:13–16; 53; Matthew 26–28; Mark 14–16; Luke 22–24; John 10:14–15; 11:25–26; 14:6; 15:13; 19–20; 1 Corinthians 15:20–22; Hebrews 4:14–16; 1 John 1:7; 1 Nephi 10:6; 2 Nephi 2:1–10; 9; 25:23–26; Jacob 4:12; Mosiah 3:1–19; Alma 22:14; 34:5–18; 42; Helaman 5:9–12; 14:13–19; 3 Nephi 9:14–22; 27:13–22; Mormon 9:10–14; Ether 12:27, 41; Moroni 8:5–26; 10:32–33; D&C 18:10–12; 19:15–24; 20:17–34; 45:3–5; 76:40–43; Moses 1:39

## Baptism

The Book of Mormon tells of a group of people who learned the gospel and were baptized at a place called Mormon. From the time of their baptism, they regarded Mormon as a place of beauty because while they were there, they "came to the knowledge of their Redeemer" (Mosiah 18:30). Strengthened by their testimonies and their baptismal covenant, they remained faithful to the Lord, even in times of intense trial (see Mosiah 23–24).

Like the people in this Book of Mormon account, you can rejoice as you remember your baptismal covenant and the Lord's promises to you. You can find strength in the ordinance of baptism, whether you were baptized recently or many years ago.

### Entering the Path to Eternal Life

Baptism is the first saving ordinance of the gospel (see Articles of Faith 1:4). Through baptism and confirmation by priesthood authority, you became a member of The Church of Jesus Christ of Latter-day Saints.

When you were baptized, you showed your willingness to follow the Savior's example. He too was baptized, even though He was without sin. As He explained to John the Baptist, He needed to be baptized in order to "fulfil all righteousness" (see Matthew 3:13–17).

All who seek eternal life must follow the example of the Savior by being baptized and receiving the gift of the Holy Ghost. The prophet Nephi said that the Savior showed us "the gate by which [we] should enter. For the gate by which [we] should enter is repentance and baptism by water; and then cometh a remission of [our] sins by fire and by the Holy

21

Ghost. And then are [we] in this strait and narrow path which leads to eternal life" (2 Nephi 31:17–18). We will receive eternal life if we endure to the end, keeping our covenants and receiving other ordinances of salvation.

Baptism in the Lord's Way

The Savior revealed the true method of baptism to the Prophet Joseph Smith, making clear that the ordinance must be performed by one having priesthood authority and that it must be done by immersion:

"The person who is called of God and has authority from Jesus Christ to baptize, shall go down into the water with the person who has presented himself or herself for baptism, and shall say, calling him or her by name: Having been commissioned of Jesus Christ, I baptize you in the name of the Father, and of the Son, and of the Holy Ghost. Amen.

"Then shall he immerse him or her in the water, and come forth again out of the water" (D&C 20:73–74).

Immersion is symbolic of the death of a person's sinful life and the rebirth into a spiritual life, dedicated to the service of God and His children. It is also symbolic of death and resurrection. (See Romans 6:3–6.)

Little Children and Baptism

From latter-day revelation, we know that little children are redeemed through the mercy of Jesus Christ. The Lord said, "They cannot sin, for power is not given unto Satan to tempt little children, until they begin to become accountable before me" (see D&C 29:46–47). They are not to be baptized until they reach the age of accountability, which the Lord has revealed to be eight years of age (see D&C 68:27; Joseph Smith Translation, Genesis 17:11). Anyone who claims that little children need baptism "denieth the mercies of Christ, and setteth at naught the atonement of him and the power of his redemption" (Moroni 8:20; see also verses 8–19, 21–24).

Your Baptismal Covenant

When you were baptized, you entered into a covenant with God. You promised to take upon yourself the name of Jesus Christ, keep His commandments, and serve Him to the end (see Mosiah 18:8–10; D&C 20:37). You renew this covenant each time you partake of the sacrament (see D&C 20:77, 79).

*Taking upon Yourself the Name of Jesus Christ.* When you take upon yourself the name of Jesus Christ, you see yourself as His. You put Him and His work first in your life. You seek what He wants rather than what you want or what the world teaches you to want.

In the Book of Mormon, King Benjamin explains why it is important to take the name of the Savior upon ourselves:

"There is no other name given whereby salvation cometh; therefore, I would that ye should take upon you the name of Christ, all you that have entered into the covenant with God that ye should be obedient unto the end of your lives.

"And it shall come to pass that whosoever doeth this shall be found at the right hand of God, for he shall know the name by which he is called; for he shall be called by the name of Christ.

"And now it shall come to pass, that whosoever shall not take upon him the name of Christ must be called by some other name; therefore, he findeth himself on the left hand of God" (Mosiah 5:8–10).

*Keeping the Commandments.* Your baptismal covenant is a commitment to come into God's kingdom, separating yourself from the world and standing as a witness of God "at all times and in all things, and in all places" (Mosiah 18:9). Your efforts to stand as a witness of God include everything you do and say. Strive always to remember and keep the Lord's commandments. Keep your thoughts, language, and actions pure. When you seek entertainment such as movies, television, the Internet, music, books, magazines, and newspapers, be careful to watch, listen to, and read only those things that are uplifting. Dress modestly. Choose friends who encourage you to reach your eternal goals. Stay away from immorality, pornography, gambling, tobacco, alcohol, and illicit drugs. Keep yourself worthy to enter the temple.

*Serving the Lord.* The commandment to separate yourself from the things of the world does not mean that you should isolate yourself from others. Part of the baptismal covenant is to serve the Lord, and you serve Him best when you serve your fellow men. When the prophet Alma taught about the baptismal covenant, he said that we should be "willing to bear one another's burdens, that they may be light" and "willing to mourn with those that mourn . . . and comfort those that stand in need of comfort" (Mosiah 18:8–9). Be kind and respectful to all people, following the example of Jesus Christ in the way you treat others.

Promised Blessings of Baptism

As you keep the covenant you made at baptism, the Lord will bless you for your faithfulness. Some of the blessings you receive are the constant companionship of the Holy Ghost, the remission of your sins, and the privilege of being spiritually reborn.

*The Constant Companionship of the Holy Ghost.* After you were baptized, one or more authorized Melchizedek Priesthood holders laid their hands on your head and gave you the gift of the Holy Ghost. This gift gives you the right to the constant companionship of the Holy Ghost as long as you are worthy. The Spirit's constant companionship is one of the greatest blessings you can receive in mortality. The Spirit will guide you in the paths of righteousness and peace, leading you to eternal life.

*Remission of Sins.* Because you have been baptized, you can receive a remission of your sins. In other words, you can be forgiven through the mercy of the Savior. With this blessing, you can be permitted eventually to live in the presence of Heavenly Father.

To receive a remission of your sins, you must exercise faith in Jesus Christ, be sincerely repentant, and strive always to keep the commandments. The prophet Mormon taught, "The first fruits of repentance is baptism; and baptism cometh by faith unto the fulfilling the commandments; and the fulfilling the commandments bringeth remission of sins" (Moroni 8:25). You "retain a remission of your sins" as you continue to humble yourself before God, call upon Him daily in prayer, remain steadfast in the faith, and serve those in need (see Mosiah 4:11–12, 26).

*Being Born Again.* Through the ordinances of baptism and confirmation, you were born again into a new life. The Savior said to Nicodemus, "Except a man be born of water and of the Spirit, he cannot enter into the kingdom of God" (John 3:5). Just as an infant enters a new existence at birth, you began a new life when you entered into the baptismal covenant. You can grow in spirituality and become more like the Savior by keeping your baptismal covenant, partaking of the sacrament to renew your covenant, and repenting of your sins. The Apostle Paul taught that when we have been baptized, we "should walk in newness of life" (Romans 6:4).

Enduring to the End

Now that you are baptized and have received the gift of the Holy Ghost, you must continue in righteousness, for these ordinances mark only the beginning of your journey back to dwell with your Heavenly Father. The prophet Nephi taught:

"After ye have gotten into this strait and narrow path, I would ask if all is done? Behold, I say unto you, Nay; for ye have not come thus far save it were by the word of Christ with unshaken faith in him, relying wholly upon the merits of him who is mighty to save.

"Wherefore, ye must press forward with a steadfastness in Christ, having a perfect brightness of hope, and a love of God and of all men. Wherefore, if ye shall press forward, feasting upon the word of Christ, and endure to the end, behold, thus saith the Father: Ye shall have eternal life" (2 Nephi 31:19–20).

Additional references: Acts 2:37–38; 2 Nephi 31:4–13; Alma 7:14–16; 3 Nephi 11:18–41; 27:13–22; D&C 39:5–6, 10; 76:50–53

*See also* Faith; Holy Ghost; Obedience; Priesthood; Repentance; Sacrament

**Bible** (*See* Scriptures)

## Birth Control

When married couples are physically able, they have the privilege of providing mortal bodies for Heavenly Father's spirit children. They play a part in the great plan of happiness, which permits God's children to receive physical bodies and experience mortality.

If you are married, you and your spouse should discuss your sacred responsibility to bring children into the world and nurture them in righteousness. As you do so, consider the sanctity and meaning of life. Ponder the joy that comes when children are in the home. Consider the eternal blessings that come from having a good posterity. With a testimony of these principles, you and your spouse will be prepared to prayerfully decide how many children to have and when to have them. Such decisions are between the two of you and the Lord.

As you discuss this sacred matter, remember that sexual relations within marriage are divinely approved. While one purpose of these relations is to provide physical bodies for God's children, another purpose is to express love for one another—to bind husband and wife together in loyalty, fidelity, consideration, and common purpose.

**Bishop** (*See* Church Administration)

## Body Piercing

Latter-day prophets strongly discourage the piercing of the body except for medical purposes. If girls or women desire to have their ears pierced, they are encouraged to wear only one pair of modest earrings.

Those who choose to disregard this counsel show a lack of respect for themselves and for God. They will someday regret their decision.

The Apostle Paul taught of the significance of our bodies and the danger of purposefully defiling them: "Know ye not that ye are the temple of God, and that the Spirit of God dwelleth in you? If any man defile the temple of God, him shall God destroy; for the temple of God is holy, which temple ye are" (1 Corinthians 3:16–17).

*See also* Modesty; Tattooing

## **Book of Mormon** (*See* Scriptures)

## **Born Again** (*See* Baptism; Conversion; Salvation)

## **Celestial Kingdom** (*See* Kingdoms of Glory)

## Charity

Charity is "the pure love of Christ," or "everlasting love" (Moroni 7:47; 8:17). The prophet Mormon taught: "Charity suffereth long, and is kind, and envieth not, and is not puffed up, seeketh not her own, is not easily provoked, thinketh no evil, and rejoiceth not in iniquity but rejoiceth in the truth, beareth all things, believeth all things, hopeth all things, endureth all things" (Moroni 7:45; see also 1 Corinthians 13:4–7).

Jesus Christ is the perfect example of charity. In His mortal ministry, He always "went about doing good," teaching the gospel and showing tender compassion for the poor, afflicted, and distressed (see Matthew 4:23; Mark 6:6; Acts 10:38). His crowning expression of charity was His infinite Atonement. He said, "Greater love hath no man than this, that a man lay down his life for his friends" (John 15:13). This was the greatest act of long-suffering, kindness, and selflessness that we will ever know. With an understanding of the Savior's enduring love, you can exercise faith and repent of your sins, confident that He will forgive you and strengthen you in your efforts to live the gospel.

The Savior wants you to receive His love, and He also wants you to share it with others. He declared to His disciples: "A new commandment I give unto you, That ye love one another; as I have loved you, that ye also love one another. By this shall all men know that ye are my disciples, if ye have love one to another" (John 13:34–35). In your relationships with family members and others, look to the Savior as your example. Strive to love as He loves, with unfailing compassion, patience, and mercy.

As you continue to receive the Savior's perfect love and as you demonstrate Christlike love for others, you will find that your love increases. You will experience the joy of being in the Lord's service. The Holy Ghost will be your constant companion, guiding you in your service and in your relationships with others. You will be prepared to meet the Lord at the Judgment, when He will reward you according to your dedication to His work. Mormon taught:

"If ye have not charity, ye are nothing, for charity never faileth. Wherefore, cleave unto charity, which is the greatest of all, for all things must fail—

"But charity is the pure love of Christ, and it endureth forever; and whoso is found possessed of it at the last day, it shall be well with him.

"Wherefore, my beloved brethren, pray unto the Father with all the energy of heart, that ye may be filled with this love, which he hath bestowed upon all who are true followers of his Son, Jesus Christ; that ye may become the sons of God; that when he shall appear we shall be like him, for we shall see him as he is; that we may have this hope; that we may be purified even as he is pure" (Moroni 7:46–48).

Additional references: Matthew 25:31–46; 1 John 4:18; Ether 12:33–34; D&C 12:8; 34:3; 121:45

*See also* Love; Service

## Chastity

Chastity is sexual purity, a condition that is "pleasing unto God" (Jacob 2:7). To be chaste, you must be morally clean in your thoughts, words, and actions. You must not have any sexual relations before you are legally married. When you are married, you must be completely faithful to your husband or wife.

Physical intimacy between husband and wife is beautiful and sacred. It is ordained of God for the creation of children and for the expression of love within marriage.

In the world today, Satan has led many people to believe that sexual intimacy outside of marriage is acceptable. But in God's sight, it is a serious sin. It is an abuse of the power He has given us to create life. The prophet Alma taught that sexual sins are more serious than any other sins except murder and denying the Holy Ghost (see Alma 39:3–5).

Sometimes people try to convince themselves that sexual relations outside of marriage are acceptable if the participants love one another. This is not true. Breaking the law of chastity and encouraging someone else to do so is not an expression of love. People who love each other will never endanger one another's happiness and safety in exchange for temporary personal pleasure.

When people care for one another enough to keep the law of chastity, their love, trust, and commitment increase, resulting in greater happiness and unity. In contrast, relationships built on sexual immorality sour quickly. Those who engage in sexual immorality often feel fear, guilt, and shame. Bitterness, jealousy, and hatred soon replace any positive feelings that once existed in their relationship.

Our Heavenly Father has given us the law of chastity for our protection. Obedience to this law is essential to personal peace and strength of character and to happiness in the home. As you keep yourself sexually pure, you will avoid the spiritual and emotional damage that always come from sharing physical intimacies with someone outside of marriage. You will be sensitive to the Holy Ghost's guidance, strength, comfort, and protection, and you will fulfill an important requirement for receiving a temple recommend and participating in temple ordinances.

## Sexual Sins

The Lord and His prophets condemn sexual immorality. All sexual relations outside of marriage violate the law of chastity and are physically and spiritually dangerous for those who engage in them.

The Ten Commandments include the command that we not commit adultery, which is sexual intercourse between a married man and someone other than his wife or between a married woman and someone other than her husband (see Exodus 20:14). The Apostle Paul said that it is "the will of God" that we "abstain from fornication," which is sexual intercourse between an unmarried person and anyone else (1 Thessalonians 4:3). Latter-day prophets repeatedly speak out against these sins and against the evil practice of sexual abuse.

Like other violations of the law of chastity, homosexual activity is a serious sin. It is contrary to the purposes of human sexuality (see Romans 1:24–32). It distorts loving relationships and prevents people from receiving the blessings that can be found in family life and the saving ordinances of the gospel.

Merely refraining from sexual intercourse outside of marriage is not sufficient in the Lord's standard of personal purity. The Lord requires a high moral standard of His disciples, including complete fidelity to one's spouse in thought and conduct. In the Sermon on the Mount, He said: "Ye have heard that it was said by them of old time, Thou shalt not commit adultery: But I say unto you, That whosoever looketh on a woman to lust after her hath committed adultery with her already in his heart" (Matthew 5:27–28). In the latter days He has said, "Thou shalt not . . . commit adultery, . . . nor do anything like unto it" (D&C 59:6). And He has reemphasized the principle He taught in the Sermon on the Mount: "He that looketh on a woman to lust after her, or if any shall commit adultery in their hearts, they shall not have the Spirit, but shall deny the faith and shall fear" (D&C 63:16). These warnings apply to all people, whether they are married or single.

If you have committed sexual sin, speak with your bishop or branch president so he can help you through the process of repentance (see "Repentance," pages 132–35).

If you find yourself struggling with sexual temptations, including feelings of same-gender attraction, do not give in to those temptations. Be assured that you can choose to avoid such behavior. You can receive the Lord's help as you pray for strength and work to overcome the problem. As part of this process, you should seek counsel from your bishop or branch president. He will help you.

## Keeping the Law of Chastity

No matter how strong temptations seem, the Lord will help you withstand them if you choose to follow Him. The Apostle Paul declared, "There hath no temptation taken you but such as is common to man: but God is faithful, who will not suffer you to be tempted above that ye are able; but will with the temptation also make a way to escape, that ye

31

may be able to bear it" (1 Corinthians 10:13). The following counsel can help you overcome the frequent and blatant temptations in the world today:

*Decide now to be chaste.* You need to make this decision only once. Make the decision now, before the temptation comes, and let your decision be so firm and with such deep commitment that it can never be shaken. Determine now that you will never do anything outside of marriage to arouse the powerful emotions that must be expressed only in marriage. Do not arouse those emotions in another person's body or in your own body. Determine now that you will be completely true to your spouse.

*Control your thoughts.* No one commits sexual sin in an instant. Immoral acts always begin with impure thoughts. If you allow your thoughts to linger on obscene or immoral things, you have already taken the first step toward immorality. Flee immediately from situations that may lead to sin. Pray for constant strength to resist temptation and control your thoughts. Make this a part of your daily prayers.

*Stay away from pornography.* Do not view, read, or listen to anything that depicts or describes the human body or sexual conduct in a way that can arouse sexual feelings. Pornographic materials are addictive and destructive. They can rob you of your self-respect and of a sense of the beauties of life. They can tear you down and lead you to evil thoughts and abusive conduct.

*If you are single and dating, always treat your date with respect.* Never treat him or her as an object to be used for lustful desires. Carefully plan positive and constructive activities so that you and your date are not left alone without anything to do. Stay in areas of safety where you can easily control yourself. Do not participate in conversations or activities that arouse sexual feelings. Do not participate in passionate kissing, lie with or on top of another person, or touch the private, sacred parts of another person's body, with or without clothing. Do not allow anyone to do such things with you.

*If you are married, be faithful to your spouse in your thoughts, words, and actions.* The Lord has said: "Thou shalt love thy wife with all thy heart, and shalt cleave unto her and none else. And he that looketh upon a woman to lust after her shall deny the faith, and shall not have the Spirit; and if he repents not he shall be cast out" (D&C 42:22–23). Never flirt in any way. As much as possible, avoid being alone with anyone of the opposite sex. Ask yourself if your spouse would be pleased if he or she knew of your words or actions. Remember the Apostle Paul's counsel to "abstain from all appearance of evil" (1 Thessalonians 5:22). When you stay away from such circumstances, temptation gets no chance to develop.

## Forgiveness for the Repentant

The best course is complete moral cleanliness. It is wrong to commit sexual sins with the thought that you will simply repent later. This attitude is a sin itself, showing irreverence for the Lord and the covenants you make with Him. However, if you have committed sexual sins, the Lord offers forgiveness if you repent.

Repentance is difficult, but it is possible. You can be clean again (see Isaiah 1:18). The despair of sin can be replaced with the sweet peace of forgiveness. To learn what you must do to repent, see "Repentance," pages 132–35.

Work toward the day when you will be worthy to enter the temple, guided by the words of the Psalmist:

"Who shall ascend into the hill of the Lord? or who shall stand in his holy place?

"He that hath clean hands, and a pure heart" (Psalm 24:3–4).

Additional references: Exodus 20:14; 1 Corinthians 6:18–20; Alma 38:12; 3 Nephi 12:27–30

*See also* Marriage; Pornography

## Church Administration

Jesus Christ stands at the head of the Church. The mission of The Church of Jesus Christ of Latter-day Saints is to help all people come unto Him (see Moroni 10:32). To fulfill this mission, the Church is organized according to the pattern revealed by the Lord "for the perfecting of the saints, . . . till we all come in the unity of the faith, and of the knowledge of the Son of God" (Ephesians 4:12–13; see also verse 11). The following outline summarizes the organization of the Church.

### Home and Family

The family is the fundamental unit in the Church, and home is the most important place for gospel learning. No other organization can take the place of the family. Even as the Church continues to grow, its purpose will always be to support and strengthen families and individuals in their efforts to live the gospel.

### General Administration

The Lord guides His covenant people today through the President of the Church, whom we sustain as prophet, seer, and revelator. The President of the Church presides over the entire Church. He and his counselors, who are also prophets, seers, and revelators, form the Quorum of the First Presidency.

Members of the Quorum of the Twelve Apostles are also prophets, seers, and revelators. They, along with the First Presidency, are "special witnesses of the name of Christ in all the world" (D&C 107:23). They act under the direction of the First Presidency "to build up the church, and regulate all the affairs of the same in all nations" (D&C 107:33). They "open the door [to the nations] by the proclamation of the gospel of Jesus Christ" (D&C 107:35).

Members of the Quorums of the Seventy are called to proclaim the gospel and build up the Church. They work under the direction of the Twelve Apostles and the leadership of seven brethren who are called to serve as the Presidency of the Seventy. Members of the First and Second Quorums of the Seventy are designated General Authorities, and they may be called to serve anywhere in the world.

The Presiding Bishopric is the presidency of the Aaronic Priesthood throughout the Church. The Presiding Bishop and his counselors serve under the direction of the First Presidency to administer the temporal affairs of the Church.

The Young Men, Relief Society, Young Women, Primary, and Sunday School organizations all have presidencies on the general level to provide instruction and direction.

Area Administration

An area is the largest geographic division of the Church. The First Presidency assigns the Presidency of the Seventy to directly supervise selected areas of the Church under the direction of the Quorum of the Twelve Apostles. In other areas of the Church, the First Presidency assigns Area Presidencies to preside. An Area Presidency consists of a president, who is usually assigned from the First or Second Quorum of the Seventy, and two counselors, who may be assigned from any Quorum of the Seventy. Area Presidencies serve under the direction of the First Presidency, the Quorum of the Twelve, and the Presidency of the Seventy.

Some brethren are ordained to the office of Seventy but do not serve as General Authorities. They are called Area Authority Seventies, and they are assigned to quorums other than the First or Second Quorums of the Seventy, according to geographic location. Their jurisdiction is limited to the general region in which they live. Some Area Authority Seventies serve in Area Presidencies.

Local Administration

*Wards and Branches.* Members of the Church are organized into congregations that meet together frequently for spiritual and social enrichment. Large congregations are called

35

wards. Each ward is presided over by a bishop, assisted by two counselors.

Small congregations are called branches. Each branch is presided over by a branch president, assisted by two counselors. A branch may be organized when at least two member families live in an area and one of the members is a worthy Melchizedek Priesthood holder or a worthy priest in the Aaronic Priesthood. A stake, mission, or district presidency organizes and supervises the branch. A branch can develop into a ward if it is located within a stake.

Each ward or branch comprises a specific geographic area. Different organizations in the ward or branch contribute to the Lord's work: high priests groups; elders quorums; the Relief Society, for women ages 18 years and older; Aaronic Priesthood quorums, for young men ages 12 through 17; the Young Women program, for young women ages 12 through 17; Primary, for children ages 18 months to 11 years; and the Sunday School, for all Church members ages 12 and older. Each of these organizations fulfills important roles in teaching the gospel, giving service, and supporting parents in their sacred duty to help their children become converted to the gospel of Jesus Christ. These organizations also work together to help members share the gospel with others.

*Stakes, Missions, and Districts.* Most geographic areas where the Church is organized are divided into stakes. The term *stake* comes from the prophet Isaiah, who prophesied that the latter-day Church would be like a tent, held secure by stakes (see Isaiah 33:20; 54:2). There are usually 5 to 12 wards and branches in a stake. Each stake is presided over by a stake president, assisted by two counselors. Stake presidents report to and receive direction from the Presidency of the Seventy or the Area Presidency.

A mission is a unit of the Church that normally covers an area much larger than that covered by a stake. Each mission is presided over by a mission president, assisted by two counselors. Mission presidents are directly accountable to General Authorities.

Just as a branch is a smaller version of a ward, a district is a smaller version of a stake. A district is organized when there are a sufficient number of branches located in an area, permitting easy communication and convenient travel to district meetings. A district president is called to preside over it, with the help of two counselors. The district president reports to the mission presidency. A district can develop into a stake.

*Programs for Single Members.* Many Church members have never married or are divorced or widowed. These members comprise two groups: young single adults (ages 18 through 30) and single adults (ages 31 and older).

There is not a Churchwide program for young single adults and single adults. Instead, when enough single members live in an area, local priesthood leaders are encouraged to call single-member representatives, who work under their direction. Single-member representatives plan activities such as dances, service projects, and firesides. These activities give single members opportunities to meet with and strengthen one another. Single members are also encouraged to meet regularly with their priesthood leaders to discuss their needs and their opportunities for spiritual growth and service.

Additional reference: D&C 107

*See also* Priesthood; Relief Society

## Church Disciplinary Councils

Bishops and branch presidents and stake, mission, and district presidents have a responsibility to help members overcome transgression through repentance. The most serious transgressions, such as serious violations of civil law, spouse abuse, child abuse, adultery, fornication, rape, and incest, often require formal Church discipline. Formal Church discipline may include restriction of Church membership privileges or loss of Church membership.

The process of formal discipline begins when a presiding priesthood leader calls for a disciplinary council. The purposes of disciplinary councils are to save the souls of transgressors, protect the innocent, and safeguard the purity, integrity, and good name of the Church.

Church discipline is an inspired process that takes place over a period of time. Through this process and through the Atonement of Jesus Christ, a member can receive forgiveness of sins, regain peace of mind, and gain strength to avoid transgression in the future. Church disciplinary action is not intended to be the end of the process. It is designed to help Heavenly Father's children continue in their efforts to return to full fellowship and the full blessings of the Church. The desired result is that the person make whatever changes are necessary to repent completely.

*See also* Forgiveness; Repentance

## Civil Government and Law

Section 134 of the Doctrine and Covenants outlines Latter-day Saints' "belief with regard to earthly governments and laws in general" (D&C 134, section heading). The section includes the following statements:

"We believe that governments were instituted of God for the benefit of man; and that he holds men accountable for their acts in relation to them, both in making laws and administering them, for the good and safety of society. . . .

"We believe that all men are bound to sustain and uphold the respective governments in which they reside, while protected in their inherent and inalienable rights by the laws of such governments; and that sedition and rebellion are unbecoming every citizen thus protected, and should be punished accordingly; and that all governments have a right to enact such laws as in their own judgments are best calculated to secure the public interest; at the same time, however, holding sacred the freedom of conscience.

"We believe that every man should be honored in his station, rulers and magistrates as such, being placed for the protection of the innocent and the punishment of the guilty; and that to the laws all men show respect and deference, as without them peace and harmony would be supplanted by anarchy and terror; human laws being instituted for the express purpose of regulating our interests as individuals and nations, between man and man; and divine laws given of heaven, prescribing rules on spiritual concerns, for faith and worship, both to be answered by man to his Maker" (D&C 134:1, 5–6).

One key element of the separation of church and state is the government's responsibility to grant freedom of religion. Latter-day prophets support this principle, as stated in the eleventh article of faith: "We claim the privilege of worshiping Almighty God according to the dictates of our own conscience, and allow all men the same privilege, let them worship how, where, or what they may." Consistent with the separation of church and state, the Church does not endorse any political party or candidate. It does not permit the use of its buildings and facilities for political purposes. The Church does not participate in politics unless there is a moral question at issue, in which case the Church will often speak out.

Although the Church remains politically neutral, Church leaders encourage individual members to be involved as citizens. As a Latter-day Saint, you should understand your place and position in the land in which you live. Learn about the history, heritage, and laws of the land. If you have the opportunity to vote and to participate in the affairs of government, be actively engaged in supporting and defending the principles of truth, righteousness, and freedom.

Additional references: D&C 98:10; Articles of Faith 1:12

**Coffee** (*See* Word of Wisdom)

**Comforter** (*See* Holy Ghost)

**Confirmation** (*See* Holy Ghost; Laying On of Hands)

## Conscience

All people are born with the capacity to distinguish between right and wrong. This ability, called conscience, is a manifestation of the Light of Christ (see Moroni 7:15–19).

Your conscience is a defense to help you stay away from situations that are spiritually harmful. When you obey the commandments and make righteous decisions, you experience peace of conscience.

When you sin, you feel remorse or guilt, just as you feel physical pain when you are wounded. This is the natural response of your conscience to sin, and it can lead you to repent.

Repentance and forgiveness renew your peace of conscience. On the other hand, if you ignore your conscience and do not repent, your conscience will be impaired as if it has been "seared with a hot iron" (1 Timothy 4:2).

Learn to follow your conscience. This is an important part of exercising your agency. The more you follow your conscience, the stronger it will become. A sensitive conscience is a sign of a healthy spirit.

Additional references: Mosiah 4:1–3; D&C 84:45–47

*See also* Agency; Light of Christ; Obedience; Temptation

**Contributions** (*See* Fasting and Fast Offerings; Tithing)

## Conversion

"To be carnally minded is death," declared the Apostle Paul, "but to be spiritually minded is life and peace" (Romans 8:6; see also 2 Nephi 9:39). In our fallen state, we often struggle with temptation, and we sometimes give in to "the will of the flesh and the evil which is therein" (2 Nephi 2:29; see also "Fall," pages 56–59 in this book). To be able to receive the blessing of eternal life, we need to be "spiritually minded" and conquer our unrighteous desires. We need to change. More accurately, we need to *be changed,* or converted, through the power of the Savior's Atonement and through the power of the Holy Ghost. This process is called conversion.

Conversion includes a change in behavior, but it goes beyond behavior; it is a change in our very nature. It is such a significant change that the Lord and His prophets refer to it as a rebirth, a change of heart, and a baptism of fire. The Lord said:

"Marvel not that all mankind, yea, men and women, all nations, kindreds, tongues and people, must be born again; yea, born of God, changed from their carnal and fallen state, to a state of righteousness, being redeemed of God, becoming his sons and daughters;

"And thus they become new creatures; and unless they do this, they can in nowise inherit the kingdom of God" (Mosiah 27:25–26).

## The Process of Conversion

Conversion is a process, not an event. You become converted as a result of your righteous efforts to follow the Savior. These efforts include exercising faith in Jesus Christ, repenting of sin, being baptized, receiving the gift of the Holy Ghost, and enduring to the end in faith.

Although conversion is miraculous and life changing, it is a quiet miracle. Angelic visitations and other spectacular occurrences do not bring conversion. Even Alma, who saw an angel, became converted only after he "fasted and prayed many days" for a witness of the truth (Alma 5:46). And Paul, who saw the resurrected Savior, taught that "no man can say that Jesus is the Lord, but by the Holy Ghost" (1 Corinthians 12:3).

Because conversion is a quiet, constant process, you may be converted now and not realize it. You could be like the Lamanites who, "because of their faith in [Christ] at the time

41

of their conversion, were baptized with fire and with the Holy Ghost, and they knew it not" (3 Nephi 9:20). Your continuing efforts to exercise faith and follow the Savior will lead to greater conversion.

## Characteristics of People Who Are Converted

The Book of Mormon provides descriptions of people who are converted to the Lord:

*They desire to do good.* King Benjamin's people declared, "The Spirit of the Lord Omnipotent, . . . has wrought a mighty change in us, or in our hearts, that we have no more disposition to do evil, but to do good continually" (Mosiah 5:2). Alma spoke of people who "could not look upon sin save it were with abhorrence" (Alma 13:12).

*They do not rebel against the Lord.* Mormon told of a group of Lamanites who had been wicked and bloodthirsty but who were "converted unto the Lord" (Alma 23:6). These people changed their name to the Anti-Nephi-Lehies and "became a righteous people; they did lay down the weapons of their rebellion, that they did not fight against God any more, neither against any of their brethren" (Alma 23:7).

*They share the gospel.* Enos, Alma the Elder, Alma the Younger, the sons of Mosiah, Amulek, and Zeezrom dedicated themselves to preaching the gospel after they became converted to the Lord (see Enos 1:26; Mosiah 18:1; Mosiah 27:32–37; Alma 10:1–12; 15:12).

*They are filled with love.* After the resurrected Savior visited the people in the Americas, "the people were all converted unto the Lord, upon all the face of the land, both Nephites and Lamanites, and there were no contentions and disputations among them, and every man did deal justly one with another. . . .

"And it came to pass that there was no contention in the land, because of the love of God which did dwell in the hearts of the people.

"And there were no envyings, nor strifes, nor tumults, nor whoredoms, nor lyings, nor murders, nor any manner of lasciviousness; and surely there could not be a happier people among all the people who had been created by the hand of God.

"There were no robbers, nor murderers, neither were there Lamanites, nor any manner of -ites; but they were in one, the children of Christ, and heirs to the kingdom of God" (4 Nephi 1:2, 15–17).

## Striving for Greater Conversion

You have primary responsibility for your own conversion. No one can be converted for you, and no one can force you to be converted. However, others can help you in the process of conversion. Learn from the righteous examples of family members, Church leaders and teachers, and men and women in the scriptures.

Your capacity to experience a mighty change of heart will increase as you strive to follow the Savior's perfect example. Study the scriptures, pray in faith, keep the commandments, and seek the constant companionship of the Holy Ghost. As you continue in the conversion process, you will receive "exceedingly great joy," as King Benjamin's people did when the Spirit "wrought a mighty change in [their] hearts" (see Mosiah 5:2, 4). You will be able to follow King Benjamin's counsel to "be steadfast and immovable, always abounding in good works, that Christ, the Lord God Omnipotent, may seal you his, that you may be brought to heaven, that ye may have everlasting salvation and eternal life" (Mosiah 5:15).

Additional references: Matthew 18:3; Luke 22:32; Alma 5:7–14

*See also* Atonement of Jesus Christ; Baptism; Holy Ghost; Salvation

## **Council in Heaven** (*See* Plan of Salvation)

## Covenant

A covenant is a sacred agreement between God and a person or group of people. God sets specific conditions, and He promises to bless us as we obey those conditions. When we choose not to keep covenants, we cannot receive the blessings, and in some instances we suffer a penalty as a consequence of our disobedience.

All the saving ordinances of the priesthood are accompanied by covenants. For example, you made a covenant when you were baptized, and you renew that covenant each time you partake of the sacrament (see Mosiah 18:8–10; D&C 20:37, 77, 79). If you have received the Melchizedek Priesthood, you have entered into the oath and covenant of the priesthood (see D&C 84:33–44). The temple endowment and the sealing ordinance also include sacred covenants.

Always remember and honor the covenants you make with the Lord. Then you will not need to be commanded in everything you do (see D&C 58:26–28). You will be inspired by the Holy Ghost, and Christlike conduct will be part of your nature. As the Lord has promised, you will "receive revelation upon revelation, knowledge upon knowledge, that thou mayest know the mysteries and peaceable things—that which bringeth joy, that which bringeth life eternal" (D&C 42:61). Your greatest hope should be to enjoy the sanctification that comes from this divine guidance; your greatest fear should be to forfeit these blessings.

Additional references: Jeremiah 31:31–34; Mosiah 5; Moroni 10:33; D&C 82:10; 97:8; 98:13–15

*See also* Abrahamic Covenant; Baptism; Marriage; Ordinances; Priesthood; Sacrament; Temples

## Creation

Under the direction of Heavenly Father, Jesus Christ created the heavens and the earth (see Mosiah 3:8; Moses 2:1).

From scripture revealed through the Prophet Joseph Smith, we know that in the work of the Creation, the Lord organized elements that had already existed (see Abraham 3:24). He did not create the world "out of nothing," as some people believe.

The scriptures also teach that Adam was "the first man of all men" (Moses 1:34). God created Adam and Eve in His own image and in the image of His Only Begotten (see Moses 2:26–27).

The Creation is an integral part of Heavenly Father's plan of salvation. It gives each of us the opportunity to come to the earth, where we receive a physical body and exercise our agency. In the premortal Council of the Gods, the following declaration was made: "We will go down, for there is space there, and we will take of these materials, and we will make an earth whereon these may dwell; and we will prove them herewith, to see if they will do all things whatsoever the Lord their God shall command them" (Abraham 3:24–25).

You are a spirit child of God, and your body is created in His image. To show your gratitude for these blessings, you can care for your body by obeying the Word of Wisdom and other commandments relating to your spiritual and physical health (see D&C 89; see also D&C 88:124). You can also respect other people as children of God.

As a beneficiary of all the beauties of creation, you can care for the earth and help preserve it for future generations.

Additional references: Genesis 1–2; Hebrews 1:1–2; 1 Nephi 17:36; D&C 38:1–3; 59:16–20; Moses 1–3; Abraham 4–5

*See also* God the Father; Jesus Christ; Plan of Salvation

## Cross

The cross is used in many Christian churches as a symbol of the Savior's death and Resurrection and as a sincere expression of faith. As members of The Church of Jesus Christ of Latter-day Saints, we also remember with reverence the suffering of the Savior. But because the Savior lives, we do not use the symbol of His death as the symbol of our faith.

Your life must be the expression of your faith. Remember that when you were baptized and confirmed, you covenanted to take upon yourself the name of Jesus Christ. As your associates observe you, they should be able to sense your love for the Savior and His work.

The only members of the Church who wear the symbol of the cross are Latter-day Saint chaplains, who wear it on their military uniforms to show that they are Christian chaplains.

*See also* Atonement of Jesus Christ; Jesus Christ; Resurrection

## Crucifixion (*See* Atonement of Jesus Christ; Cross)

## Deacon (*See* Aaronic Priesthood; Priesthood)

## Death, Physical

Physical death is the separation of the spirit from the mortal body. The Fall of Adam brought physical death into the world (see Moses 6:48).

Death is an essential part of Heavenly Father's plan of salvation (see 2 Nephi 9:6). In order to become like our Eternal Father, we must experience death and later receive perfect, resurrected bodies.

When the physical body dies, the spirit continues to live. In the spirit world, the spirits of the righteous "are received into a state of happiness, which is called paradise, a state of rest, a state of peace, where they shall rest from all their troubles and from all care, and sorrow" (Alma 40:12). A place called spirit prison is reserved for "those who [have] died in their sins, without a knowledge of the truth, or in transgression, having rejected the prophets" (D&C 138:32). The spirits in prison are "taught faith in God, repentance from sin, vicarious baptism for the remission of sins, the gift of the Holy

Ghost by the laying on of hands, and all other principles of the gospel that [are] necessary for them to know" (D&C 138:33–34). If they accept the principles of the gospel, repent of their sins, and accept ordinances performed in their behalf in temples, they will be welcomed into paradise.

Because of the Atonement and Resurrection of Jesus Christ, physical death is only temporary: "As in Adam all die, even so in Christ shall all be made alive" (1 Corinthians 15:22). Everyone will be resurrected, meaning that every person's spirit will be reunited with his or her body—"restored to their proper and perfect frame" and no longer subject to death (Alma 40:23; see also Alma 11:44–45).

You have probably experienced the pain that comes at the death of a family member or friend. It is natural to feel sorrow at such times. In fact, mourning is one of the deepest expressions of love. The Lord said, "Thou shalt live together in love, insomuch that thou shalt weep for the loss of them that die" (D&C 42:45). The only way to take sorrow out of death is to take love out of life.

Even as you mourn at the death of loved ones, you can receive comfort in the promise of resurrection and in the assurance that families can be together forever. You can "see the great reason of sorrow, and also of rejoicing—sorrow because of death and destruction among men, and joy because of the light of Christ unto life" (Alma 28:14; see also verses 9–13).

In addition to receiving comfort when loved ones die, you can be at peace with the knowledge that you will eventually die. As you live the gospel, you can remember the Lord's promise: "Those that die in me shall not taste of death, for it shall be sweet unto them" (D&C 42:46).

Additional references: Isaiah 25:8; 1 Corinthians 15:51–58; 2 Nephi 9:6–15; Mosiah 16:6–8

*See also* Atonement of Jesus Christ; Paradise; Plan of Salvation; Resurrection

## Death, Spiritual

Spiritual death is separation from God. The scriptures teach of two sources of spiritual death. The first source is the Fall, and the second is our own disobedience.

The Book of Mormon prophet Samuel taught, "All mankind, by the fall of Adam being cut off from the presence of the Lord, are considered as dead, both as to things temporal and to things spiritual" (Helaman 14:16). During our life on the earth, we are separated from God's presence. Through the Atonement, Jesus Christ redeems everyone from this spiritual death. Samuel testified that the Savior's Resurrection "redeemeth all mankind from the first death—that spiritual death. . . . Behold, the resurrection of Christ redeemeth mankind, yea, even all mankind, and bringeth them back into the presence of the Lord" (Helaman 14:16–17). The prophet Lehi taught that because of the Atonement, "all men come unto God; wherefore, they stand in the presence of him, to be judged of him according to the truth and holiness which is in him" (2 Nephi 2:10).

Further spiritual death comes as a result of our own disobedience. Our sins make us unclean and unable to dwell in the presence of God (see Romans 3:23; Alma 12:12–16, 32; Helaman 14:18; Moses 6:57). Through the Atonement, Jesus Christ offers redemption from this spiritual death, but only when we exercise faith in Him, repent of our sins, and obey the principles and ordinances of the gospel (see Alma 13:27–30; Helaman 14:19; Articles of Faith 1:3).

Additional references: 1 Nephi 15:33–35; Alma 40:26; 42:23

*See also* Atonement of Jesus Christ; Faith; Fall; Obedience; Repentance; Sin

## Debt

Through the Prophet Joseph Smith, the Lord once told a group of Saints, "It is my will that you shall pay all your debts" (D&C 104:78). Since the early days of the Church, the

Lord's prophets have warned us repeatedly to avoid the bondage of debt.

One of the great dangers of debt is the interest that accompanies it. Some forms of credit, such as credit cards, have particularly high interest rates. Once you are in debt, you find that interest has no mercy. It continues to accumulate, regardless of your situation—whether you are employed or jobless, healthy or sick. It never goes away until the debt is paid. Do not be deceived by credit offers, even if they make debt seem attractive by promising low interest rates or no interest for a certain period of time.

Look to the condition of your finances. Discipline yourself in your purchases, avoiding debt to the extent you can. In most cases, you can avoid debt by managing your resources wisely. If you do incur debt, such as a reasonable amount in order to purchase a modest home or complete your education, work to repay it as quickly as possible and free yourself from bondage. When you have paid your debts and accumulated some savings, you will be prepared for financial storms that may come your way. You will have shelter for your family and peace in your heart.

Additional references: Luke 16:10–11; D&C 19:35

## Devil (*See* Satan)

## Divorce

In "The Family: A Proclamation to the World," the First Presidency and the Quorum of the Twelve Apostles "solemnly proclaim that marriage between a man and a woman is ordained of God and that the family is central to the Creator's plan for the eternal destiny of His children" (see page 59 in this book). Despite these truths, divorce has become commonplace in many societies and has increased even among Church members. This growing plague is not of God, but rather is the work of the adversary.

Each married couple should work together to be worthy of the blessings of eternal marriage. If you are married and you and your spouse are experiencing difficulties, remember that the remedy for most marriage stress is not in divorce or separation. The remedy is found in the gospel of Jesus Christ—in repentance, forgiveness, integrity, and love. It is found in treating your spouse as you would like to be treated (see Matthew 7:12). As you work to resolve difficulties, you may want to go together to seek counsel from your bishop or branch president.

*See also* Charity; Family; Love; Marriage; Temples

## Doctrine and Covenants *(See* Scriptures)

## Drugs *(See* Word of Wisdom)

## Education

The Lord has commanded, "Seek learning, even by study and also by faith" (D&C 88:118). He has counseled us to learn the gospel and to gain an understanding "of things both in heaven and in the earth, and under the earth; things which have been, things which are, things which must shortly come to pass; things which are at home, things which are abroad; the wars and the perplexities of the nations, and the judgments which are on the land; and a knowledge also of countries and of kingdoms—that [we] may be prepared in all things" (D&C 88:78–80).

### Schooling and Professional Training

You should always work to educate your mind and your hands so you can succeed in your chosen field. Use your education to be an influence for good. As you do so, you will become known as a person of integrity. You will be prepared for opportunities as they come, and you will be a great asset to your family, the Church, and your community.

Seek the best schooling available. Some possibilities are colleges and universities, technical schools, home-study courses, community education, and private training.

## Seminary and Institute

Throughout the world, Latter-day Saints ages 14 through 18 participate in seminary, which provides weekday instruction from the scriptures. Institutes of religion provide weekday courses in a variety of gospel subjects for Latter-day Saints ages 18 through 30.

These programs provide a spiritual and social climate where students can associate with each other while learning more about the gospel.

For information about seminary and institute, contact a local priesthood leader.

## Lifelong Learning

Continue to seek opportunities for education throughout your life. This will help you stay up-to-date in your chosen profession and in your other skills and interests. In this rapidly changing world, you must make time to educate yourself for the present and the future.

In addition to furthering your education through formal schooling, you can continue learning by reading, attending wholesome cultural events, visiting museums and historic sites, and observing the world around you.

Additional references: Proverbs 1:5; D&C 130:18–19

**Elder** (*See* Melchizedek Priesthood; Priesthood)

**Endowment** (*See* Temples)

## Eternal Life

The Lord declared, "This is my work and my glory—to bring to pass the immortality and eternal life of man" (Moses 1:39). Immortality is to live forever as a resurrected being. Through the Atonement of Jesus Christ, everyone will receive this gift. Eternal life, or exaltation, is to inherit a place in the highest degree of the celestial kingdom, where we will live in God's presence and continue as families (see D&C 131:1–4). Like immortality, this gift is made possible through the Atonement of Jesus Christ. However, it requires our "obedience to the laws and ordinances of the Gospel" (Articles of Faith 1:3).

Staying on the Path to Life Eternal

When you were baptized and received the gift of the Holy Ghost, you entered the path that leads to eternal life. The prophet Nephi taught:

"The gate by which ye should enter is repentance and baptism by water; and then cometh a remission of your sins by fire and by the Holy Ghost.

"And then are ye in this strait and narrow path which leads to eternal life; yea, ye have entered in by the gate; ye have done according to the commandments of the Father and the Son; and ye have received the Holy Ghost, which witnesses of the Father and the Son, unto the fulfilling of the promise which he hath made, that if ye entered in by the way ye should receive" (2 Nephi 31:17–18).

Nephi emphasized that after we have entered this "strait and narrow path," we must endure to the end in faith:

"After ye have gotten into this strait and narrow path, I would ask if all is done? Behold, I say unto you, Nay; for ye have not come thus far save it were by the word of Christ with unshaken faith in him, relying wholly upon the merits of him who is mighty to save.

"Wherefore, ye must press forward with a steadfastness in Christ, having a perfect brightness of hope, and a love of God and of all men. Wherefore, if ye shall press forward, feasting upon the word of Christ, and endure to the end, behold, thus saith the Father: Ye shall have eternal life" (2 Nephi 31:19–20).

Now that you have been baptized and confirmed, much of your progress toward eternal life depends on your receiving other ordinances of salvation: for men, ordination to the Melchizedek Priesthood; for men and women, the temple endowment and marriage sealing. When you receive these ordinances and keep the covenants that accompany them, you prepare yourself to inherit the highest degree of celestial glory.

Within Your Reach

As you ponder your progress on the "strait and narrow path," be assured that eternal life is within your reach. The Lord wants you to return to Him, and He will never require anything of you that you cannot fulfill. All His commandments are calculated to promote your happiness. When you exercise faith and serve Him with all your might, He gives you strength and provides a way for you to do whatever He commands you (see 1 Nephi 3:7). Remember that as you give your greatest effort and repent of your sins, the Atonement of Jesus Christ will compensate for your weakness and for the inequities, injuries, and pains you experience in this life: "We know that it is by grace that we are saved, after all we can do" (2 Nephi 25:23).

Additional references: John 3:16; 17:3; 2 Nephi 9:39; Moroni 7:41; D&C 14:7; 50:5

*See also* Atonement of Jesus Christ; Grace; Kingdoms of Glory

**Exaltation** (*See* Eternal Life)

## Faith

The Apostle Paul taught that "faith is the assurance of things hoped for, the evidence of things not seen" (Hebrews 11:1; see footnote *b*). Alma made a similar statement: "If ye have faith ye hope for things which are not seen, which are true" (Alma 32:21).

Faith is a principle of action and power. Whenever you work toward a worthy goal, you exercise faith. You show your hope for something that you cannot yet see.

### Faith in the Lord Jesus Christ

In order for your faith to lead you to salvation, it must be centered in the Lord Jesus Christ (see Acts 4:10–12; Mosiah 3:17; Moroni 7:24–26; Articles of Faith 1:4). You can exercise faith in Christ when you have an assurance that He exists, a correct idea of His character, and a knowledge that you are striving to live according to His will.

Having faith in Jesus Christ means relying completely on Him—trusting in His infinite power, intelligence, and love. It includes believing His teachings. It means believing that even though you do not understand all things, He does. Remember that because He has experienced all your pains, afflictions, and infirmities, He knows how to help you rise above your daily difficulties (see Alma 7:11–12; D&C 122:8). He has "overcome the world" (John 16:33) and prepared the way for you to receive eternal life. He is always ready to help you as you remember His plea: "Look unto me in every thought; doubt not, fear not" (D&C 6:36).

### Living by Faith

Faith is much more than passive belief. You express your faith through action—by the way you live.

The Savior promised, "If ye will have faith in me ye shall have power to do whatsoever thing is expedient in me" (Moroni 7:33). Faith in Jesus Christ can motivate you to follow

His perfect example (see John 14:12). Your faith can lead you to do good works, obey the commandments, and repent of your sins (see James 2:18; 1 Nephi 3:7; Alma 34:17). Your faith can help you overcome temptation. Alma counseled his son Helaman, "Teach them to withstand every temptation of the devil, with their faith on the Lord Jesus Christ" (Alma 37:33).

The Lord will work mighty miracles in your life according to your faith (see 2 Nephi 26:13). Faith in Jesus Christ helps you receive spiritual and physical healing through His Atonement (see 3 Nephi 9:13–14). When times of trial come, faith can give you strength to press forward and face your hardships with courage. Even when the future seems uncertain, your faith in the Savior can give you peace (see Romans 5:1; Helaman 5:47).

Increasing Your Faith

Faith is a gift from God, but you must nurture your faith to keep it strong. Faith is like the muscle of your arm. If you exercise it, it grows strong. If you put it in a sling and leave it there, it becomes weak.

You can nurture the gift of faith by praying to Heavenly Father in the name of Jesus Christ. As you express your gratitude to your Father and as you plead with Him for blessings that you and others need, you will draw near to Him. You will draw near to the Savior, whose Atonement makes it possible for you to plead for mercy (see Alma 33:11). You will also be receptive to the quiet guidance of the Holy Ghost.

You can strengthen your faith by keeping the commandments. Like all blessings from God, faith is obtained and increased through individual obedience and righteous action. If you desire to enrich your faith to the highest possible degree, you must keep the covenants you have made.

You can also develop your faith by studying the scriptures and the words of latter-day prophets. The prophet Alma taught that the word of God helps strengthen faith. Comparing the word to a seed, he said that the "desire to believe" can lead you to "give place" for the word to be "planted in your heart." Then you will feel that the word is good, for it will begin to enlarge your soul and enlighten your understanding. This will strengthen your faith. As you continually nurture the word in your heart, "with great diligence, and with patience, looking forward to the fruit thereof, it shall take root; and behold it shall be a tree springing up unto everlasting life." (See Alma 32:26–43.)

Additional references: Hebrews 11; James 1:5–6; 2:14–26; Ether 12:4–27; Moroni 7:20–48; D&C 63:7–11; 90:24

*See also* Baptism; God the Father; Jesus Christ; Repentance

## Fall

In the Garden of Eden, God commanded, "Of every tree of the garden thou mayest freely eat, but of the tree of the knowledge of good and evil, thou shalt not eat of it, nevertheless, thou mayest choose for thyself, for it is given unto thee; but, remember that I forbid it, for in the day thou eatest thereof thou shalt surely die" (Moses 3:16–17). Because Adam and Eve transgressed this command and partook of the fruit of the tree of the knowledge of good and evil, they were cast out from the presence of the Lord (see D&C 29:40–41). In other words, they experienced spiritual death. They also became mortal—subject to physical death. This spiritual and physical death is called the Fall.

### Our Fallen Condition

As descendants of Adam and Eve, we inherit a fallen condition during mortality (see Alma 42:5–9, 14). We are separated from the presence of the Lord and subject to physical death. We are also placed in a state of opposition, in which we are tested by the difficulties of life and the temptations of the adversary (see 2 Nephi 2:11–14; D&C 29:39; Moses 6:48–49).

In this fallen condition, we have a conflict within us. We are spirit children of God, with the potential to be "partakers of the divine nature" (2 Peter 1:4). However, "we are unworthy before [God]; because of the fall our natures have become evil continually" (Ether 3:2). We need to strive continually to overcome unrighteous passions and desires.

Repeating the words of an angel, King Benjamin said, "The natural man is an enemy to God, and has been from the fall of Adam." King Benjamin warned that in this natural, or fallen, state, each person will be an enemy to God forever "unless he yields to the enticings of the Holy Spirit, and putteth off the natural man and becometh a saint through the atonement of Christ the Lord, and becometh as a child, submissive, meek, humble, patient, full of love, willing to submit to all things which the Lord seeth fit to inflict upon him, even as a child doth submit to his father" (Mosiah 3:19).

## Benefits of the Fall

The Fall is an integral part of Heavenly Father's plan of salvation (see 2 Nephi 2:15–16; 9:6). It has a twofold direction—downward yet forward. In addition to introducing physical and spiritual death, it gave us the opportunity to be born on the earth and to learn and progress. Through our righteous exercise of agency and our sincere repentance when we sin, we can come unto Christ and, through His Atonement, prepare to receive the gift of eternal life. The prophet Lehi taught:

"If Adam had not transgressed he would not have fallen, but he would have remained in the garden of Eden. And all things which were created must have remained in the same state in which they were after they were created; and they must have remained forever, and had no end.

"And [Adam and Eve] would have had no children; wherefore they would have remained in a state of innocence, having no joy, for they knew no misery; doing no good, for they knew no sin.

"But behold, all things have been done in the wisdom of him who knoweth all things.

"Adam fell that men might be; and men are, that they might have joy.

"And the Messiah cometh in the fulness of time, that he may redeem the children of men from the fall" (2 Nephi 2:22–26; see also verses 19–21, 27).

Adam and Eve expressed their gratitude for the blessings that came as a result of the Fall:

"Adam blessed God and was filled, and began to prophesy concerning all the families of the earth, saying: Blessed be the name of God, for because of my transgression my eyes are opened, and in this life I shall have joy, and again in the flesh I shall see God.

"And Eve, his wife, heard all these things and was glad, saying: Were it not for our transgression we never should have had seed, and never should have known good and evil, and the joy of our redemption, and the eternal life which God giveth unto all the obedient" (Moses 5:10–11).

Redemption from the Fall

Because of our fallen, mortal nature and our individual sins, our only hope is in Jesus Christ and the plan of redemption.

Through the Atonement of Jesus Christ, everyone will be redeemed from the effects of the Fall. We will be resurrected, and we will be brought back into the presence of the Lord to be judged (see 2 Nephi 2:5–10; Alma 11:42–45; Helaman 14:15–17).

In addition to redeeming us from the universal effects of the Fall, the Savior can redeem us from our own sins. In our fallen state, we sin and distance ourselves from the Lord, bringing spiritual death upon ourselves. As the Apostle Paul said, "All have sinned, and come short of the glory of God" (Romans 3:23). If we remain in our sins, we cannot dwell in the presence of God, for "no unclean thing can dwell . . . in his presence" (Moses 6:57). Thankfully, the Atonement "bringeth to pass the condition of repentance" (Helaman 14:18), making it possible for us to receive forgiveness for our sins and dwell in the presence of God forever. Alma taught, "There was a space granted unto man in which he might repent; therefore this life became a probationary state; a time to prepare to meet God; a time to prepare for that endless state which has been spoken of by us, which is after the resurrection of the dead" (Alma 12:24).

## Gratitude for the Savior's Atoning Sacrifice

Just as we do not really desire food until we are hungry, we will not fully desire eternal salvation until we recognize our need for the Savior. This recognition comes as we grow in our understanding of the Fall. As the prophet Lehi taught, "All mankind were in a lost and in a fallen state, and ever would be save they should rely on this Redeemer" (1 Nephi 10:6).

Additional references: Genesis 3; Mormon 9:12–14; Moses 4

*See also* Agency; Atonement of Jesus Christ; Original Sin; Plan of Salvation; Sin

# Family

On September 23, 1995, President Gordon B. Hinckley, the 15th President of the Church, read the following proclamation in a general Relief Society meeting. This inspired proclamation, titled "The Family: A Proclamation to the World," has become the Church's definitive statement on the family:

"We, the First Presidency and the Council of the Twelve Apostles of The Church of Jesus Christ of Latter-day Saints, solemnly proclaim that marriage between a man and a woman is ordained of God and that the family is central to the Creator's plan for the eternal destiny of His children.

"All human beings—male and female—are created in the image of God. Each is a beloved spirit son or daughter of heavenly parents, and, as such, each has a divine nature and destiny. Gender is an essential characteristic of individual premortal, mortal, and eternal identity and purpose.

"In the premortal realm, spirit sons and daughters knew and worshiped God as their Eternal Father and accepted His plan by which His children could obtain a physical body and gain earthly experience to progress toward perfection and ultimately realize his or her divine destiny as an heir of eternal life. The divine plan of happiness enables family relationships to be perpetuated beyond the grave. Sacred ordinances and covenants available in holy temples make it possible for individuals to return to the presence of God and for families to be united eternally.

"The first commandment that God gave to Adam and Eve pertained to their potential for parenthood as husband and wife. We declare that God's commandment for His children to multiply and replenish the earth remains in force. We further declare that God has commanded that the sacred powers of procreation are to be employed only between man and woman, lawfully wedded as husband and wife.

"We declare the means by which mortal life is created to be divinely appointed. We affirm the sanctity of life and of its importance in God's eternal plan.

"Husband and wife have a solemn responsibility to love and care for each other and for their children. 'Children are an heritage of the Lord' (Psalms 127:3). Parents have a sacred duty to rear their children in love and righteousness, to provide for their physical and spiritual needs, to teach them to love and serve one another, to observe the commandments of God and to be law-abiding citizens wherever they live. Husbands and wives—mothers and fathers—will be held accountable before God for the discharge of these obligations.

"The family is ordained of God. Marriage between man and woman is essential to His eternal plan. Children are entitled to birth within the bonds of matrimony, and to be reared by a father and a mother who honor marital vows with complete fidelity. Happiness in family life is most likely to be achieved when founded upon the teachings of the Lord Jesus Christ. Successful marriages and families are established and maintained on principles of faith, prayer, repentance, forgiveness, respect, love, compassion, work, and wholesome recreational activities. By divine design, fathers are to preside over their families in love and righteousness and are responsible to provide the necessities of life and protection for their families. Mothers are primarily responsible for the nurture of their children. In these sacred responsibilities, fathers and mothers are obligated to help one another as equal partners. Disability, death, or other circumstances may necessitate individual adaptation. Extended families should lend support when needed.

"We warn that individuals who violate covenants of chastity, who abuse spouse or offspring, or who fail to fulfill family responsibilities will one day stand accountable before God. Further, we warn that the disintegration of the family will bring upon individuals, communities, and nations the calamities foretold by ancient and modern prophets.

"We call upon responsible citizens and officers of government everywhere to promote those measures designed to maintain and strengthen the family as the fundamental unit of society" (*Ensign*, Nov. 1995, 102).

*See also* Family Home Evening; Marriage; Temples

## Family History Work and Genealogy

On April 3, 1836, the prophet Elijah came to Joseph Smith and Oliver Cowdery in the Kirtland Temple. He conferred upon them the sealing power of the priesthood, making it possible for families to be sealed throughout the generations. In conferring this power, he fulfilled the prophecy that the Lord would send him "to turn the hearts of the fathers to the children, and the children to the fathers" (see D&C 110:14–16; see also Malachi 4:5–6).

Through family history work, you can participate in the continuing fulfillment of this prophecy. You can learn about your ancestors and increase your love for them. You can be inspired by their stories of courage and faith. You can pass that legacy on to your children.

These are lasting benefits that come from family history work, but they are not the principal reasons for the Church's great effort to gather genealogical records. All of the Church's family history endeavors are directed to the need to form a "welding link . . . between the fathers and the children" (D&C 128:18). This welding link is formed by the power of the priesthood, through sacred temple ordinances we receive in behalf of our ancestors.

Redeeming the Dead

Many of Heavenly Father's children have died without having the opportunity to receive the fulness of the gospel. In His mercy and infinite love, the Lord has prepared a way for them to gain a testimony of the gospel and receive the saving ordinances of the priesthood.

In the spirit world, the gospel is "preached to those who [have] died in their sins, without a knowledge of the truth, or in transgression, having rejected the prophets. These [are] taught faith in God, repentance from sin, vicarious baptism for the remission of sins, the gift of the Holy Ghost by the laying on of hands, and all other principles of the gospel that [are] necessary for them to know in order to qualify themselves that they might be judged according to men in the flesh, but live according to God in the spirit" (D&C 138:32–34).

Many in the spirit world embrace the gospel. However, they cannot receive priesthood ordinances for themselves because they do not have physical bodies. In holy temples, we have the privilege of receiving ordinances in their behalf. These ordinances include baptism, confirmation, Melchizedek

Priesthood ordination (for men), the endowment, the marriage sealing, and the sealing of children to parents. The Lord revealed this work to the Prophet Joseph Smith, restoring a practice that had been revealed to Christians shortly after the Resurrection of Jesus Christ (see 1 Corinthians 15:29).

As you receive priesthood ordinances in behalf of those who have died, you become a savior on Mount Zion for them (see Obadiah 1:21). Your effort approaches the spirit of the Savior's atoning sacrifice—you perform a saving work for others that they cannot do for themselves.

Your Responsibilities in Family History Work

In family history work, you have three basic responsibilities:

1. Receive the temple ordinances for yourself and help immediate family members receive them.
2. Hold a current temple recommend and attend the temple as frequently as circumstances allow.
3. Gather family history information so you can help your ancestors receive the blessings of the temple.

You can participate in temple and family history work, at least to some extent, regardless of where you live or what your circumstances are. While you probably will not be able to do everything, you can do something. The following ideas may help you get started:

- Record important details about your own life. Record your birth date and birthplace and the dates of your baptism and confirmation. Keep a personal journal to record the highlights of your life, including personal experiences that will strengthen the faith of your children and other future generations.
- Learn about your ancestors. Begin by recording information from your memory and from accessible

sources at home. Record the vital information you accurately remember or can find about siblings, parents, uncles and aunts, grandparents, and great-grandparents. Where possible, obtain copies of certificates or other documents that include this information. As you gather more information, you may want to search in other locations, such as public records. The local ward or branch may have a family history consultant who can help you. You may also want to visit the Church's official Web site for family history, www.familysearch.org.

- As you identify your ancestors, use pedigree charts and family group forms to record the information you find. These forms are available on paper and also in Church-produced software programs, such as Personal Ancestral File.

When you have gathered the necessary information about your ancestors who have died without receiving the gospel, ensure that temple work is performed for them. Even if you do not live near enough to a temple for you and your family members to be able to do the ordinance work, you can submit ancestors' names to a temple so others can do the work for them. You may be able to visit a nearby family history center or consult with local ward or branch family history consultants to see how to do this.

The Prophet Joseph Smith declared that there are "principles in relation to the dead and the living that cannot be lightly passed over, as pertaining to our salvation. For their salvation is necessary and essential to our salvation, as . . . they without us cannot be made perfect—neither can we without our dead be made perfect" (D&C 128:15). Through your participation in family history work, you and your ancestors progress toward salvation.

*See also* Temples

## Family Home Evening

The home is the most important place for gospel learning. No other organization can take the place of the family. Latter-day prophets have repeatedly called on parents to nurture their children with love and gospel teaching.

In 1915 President Joseph F. Smith and his counselors in the First Presidency began a Churchwide effort to strengthen the family. They called on parents in the Church to gather their children once each week for a "Home Evening." Families were to take time to pray and sing together, read the scriptures, teach the gospel to one another, and participate in other activities that would build family unity.

In 1970 President Joseph Fielding Smith joined with his counselors in the First Presidency to designate Monday night as the time for family home evening. Since that announcement, the Church has kept Monday evenings free from Church activities so families can have this time together.

Latter-day prophets continue to urge Church members to give highest priority to family home evening. They have promised that our dedication to this program will help protect our families against the evils of our time and will bring us abundant joy now and throughout the eternities.

All members of the Church should make Monday evening a sacred time, reserved for family home evening. If you are married, have weekly family home evening with your spouse. As you have children, include them in family home evening. Adapt the program to their needs and interests, and let them participate. After your children grow up and move away, continue to hold family home evening with your spouse.

If you are single, consider asking your bishop or branch president to organize a home evening group for you and other single members of your ward or branch. He may call a home evening leader, who is responsible to organize the program and see that home evenings are held regularly.

A suggested outline for family home evening follows:

- Opening song
- Opening prayer
- Scripture reading
- Lesson
- Activity
- Closing song
- Closing prayer
- Refreshments

As you prepare lessons for family home evening, remember to base them on the scriptures, the teachings of latter-day prophets, and personal experiences and testimony. This book can help in selecting topics to teach. In addition, you may want to refer to other Church publications, such as the *Family Home Evening Resource Book* (item number 31106), *Gospel Principles* (31110), the *Family Guidebook* (31180), and Church magazines.

*See also* Family

**Family Prayer** (*See* Prayer)

## Fasting and Fast Offerings

To fast is to go without food and drink voluntarily for a certain period of time. Fasting combined with sincere prayer can help you prepare yourself and others to receive God's blessings.

### Purposes of Fasting

On one occasion, the Savior cast a devil out from a child and used this experience to teach His disciples about the power of prayer and fasting. His disciples asked Him, "Why could not we cast him out?" Jesus answered: "Because of your unbelief: for verily I say unto you, If ye have faith as a grain of mustard seed, ye shall say unto this mountain, Remove hence to yonder place; and it shall remove; and nothing shall be impossible unto you. Howbeit this kind goeth not out but by prayer and fasting." (See Matthew 17:14–21.)

This account teaches that prayer and fasting can give added strength to those giving and receiving priesthood blessings. The account can also be applied to your personal efforts to live the gospel. If you have a weakness or sin that you have struggled to overcome, you may need to fast and pray in order to receive the help or forgiveness you desire. Like the demon that Christ cast out, your difficulty may be the kind that will go out only through prayer and fasting.

You can fast for many purposes. Fasting is one way of worshiping God and expressing gratitude to Him (see Luke 2:37; Alma 45:1). You can fast as you ask Heavenly Father to bless the sick or afflicted (see Matthew 17:14–21). Fasting may help you and those you love receive personal revelation and become converted to the truth (see Alma 5:46; 6:6). Through fasting you can gain strength to resist temptation (see Isaiah 58:6). You can fast as you strive to humble yourself before God and exercise faith in Jesus Christ (see Omni 1:26; Helaman 3:35). You may fast to receive guidance in sharing the gospel and magnifying Church callings (see Acts 13:2–3; Alma 17:3, 9; 3 Nephi 27:1–2). Fasting may accompany righteous sorrow or mourning (see Alma 28:4–6; 30:1–2).

Fast Sunday

The Church designates one Sunday each month, usually the first Sunday, as a day of fasting. Proper observance of fast Sunday includes going without food and drink for two consecutive meals, attending fast and testimony meeting, and giving a fast offering to help care for those in need.

Your fast offering should be at least the value of the two meals you do not eat. When possible, be generous and give much more than this amount.

In addition to observing the fast days set aside by Church leaders, you can fast on any other day, according to your needs and the needs of others. However, you should not fast too frequently or for excessive periods of time.

## The True Fast

In the Sermon on the Mount, Jesus taught the true form of fasting. He spoke against hypocrites who, when they fast, "disfigure their faces, that they may appear unto men to fast." Rather than putting on an outward show of righteousness, you should fast "unto thy Father which is in secret: and thy Father, which seeth in secret, shall reward thee openly" (Matthew 6:16–18).

The prophet Isaiah also taught of the true spirit of the fast: "Is not this the fast that I have chosen? to loose the bands of wickedness, to undo the heavy burdens, and to let the oppressed go free, and that ye break every yoke? Is it not to deal thy bread to the hungry, and that thou bring the poor that are cast out to thy house? when thou seest the naked, that thou cover him; and that thou hide not thyself from thine own flesh?" (Isaiah 58:6–7).

Isaiah also testified of the blessings that come when we obey the law of the fast: "Then shall thy light break forth as the morning, and thine health shall spring forth speedily: and thy righteousness shall go before thee; the glory of the Lord shall be thy rereward. Then shalt thou call, and the Lord shall answer; thou shalt cry, and he shall say, Here I am. . . . If thou draw out thy soul to the hungry, and satisfy the afflicted soul; then shall thy light rise in obscurity, and thy darkness be as the noonday: and the Lord shall guide thee continually, and satisfy thy soul in drought, and make fat thy bones: and thou shalt be like a watered garden, and like a spring of water, whose waters fail not" (Isaiah 58:8–11).

Additional references: 3 Nephi 13:16–18; D&C 59:12–14; 88:76, 119

*See also* Prayer

**First Presidency** (*See* Church Administration; Prophets)

## Foreordination

In the premortal spirit world, God appointed certain spirits to fulfill specific missions during their mortal lives. This is called foreordination.

Foreordination does not guarantee that individuals will receive certain callings or responsibilities. Such opportunities come in this life as a result of the righteous exercise of agency, just as foreordination came as a result of righteousness in the premortal existence.

Jesus Christ was foreordained to carry out the Atonement, becoming "the Lamb slain from the foundation of the world," (Revelation 13:8; see also 1 Peter 1:19–21) The scriptures tell of others who were foreordained. The prophet Abraham learned about his foreordination when he received a vision in which he saw "many of the noble and great ones" among the spirits in the premortal spirit world. He said: "God saw these souls that they were good, and he stood in the midst of them, and he said: These I will make my rulers; for he stood among those that were spirits, and he saw that they were good; and he said unto me: Abraham, thou art one of them; thou wast chosen before thou wast born" (Abraham 3:22–23). The Lord told Jeremiah, "Before I formed thee in the belly I knew thee; and before thou camest forth out of the womb I sanctified thee, and I ordained thee a prophet unto the nations" (Jeremiah 1:5). John the Baptist was foreordained to prepare the people for the Savior's mortal ministry (see Isaiah 40:3; Luke 1:13–17; 1 Nephi 10:7–10).

The doctrine of foreordination applies to all members of the Church, not just to the Savior and His prophets. Before the creation of the earth, faithful women were given certain responsibilities and faithful men were foreordained to certain priesthood duties. Although you do not remember that time, you surely agreed to fulfill significant tasks in the service of your Father. As you prove yourself worthy, you will be given opportunities to fulfill the assignments you then received.

Additional references: Alma 13:1–9; D&C 138:53–56

*See also* Agency; Plan of Salvation

## Forgiveness

The scriptures refer to forgiveness in two ways. The Lord commands us to repent of our sins and seek His forgiveness. He also commands us to forgive those who offend or hurt us. In the Lord's prayer, Jesus counsels us to ask Heavenly Father to "forgive us our debts, as we forgive our debtors" (Matthew 6:12).

### Seeking Forgiveness from the Lord

Sin is a heavy burden. It brings the tenseness of guilt and the anguish of knowing that we have acted against the will of our Father in Heaven. It brings lingering remorse as we realize that because of our actions, we may have hurt others and prevented ourselves from receiving blessings our Father has been ready to give us.

Because of the Atonement of Jesus Christ, we can receive forgiveness for our sins through sincere and complete repentance. Sinfulness brings suffering and pain, but the Lord's forgiveness brings relief, comfort, and joy. The Lord has promised:

"Behold, he who has repented of his sins, the same is forgiven, and I, the Lord, remember them no more" (D&C 58:42).

"Though your sins be as scarlet, they shall be as white as snow; though they be red like crimson, they shall be as wool" (Isaiah 1:18).

You can experience this miracle, whether you need to repent of serious sins or day-to-day weaknesses. Just as the Savior pleaded with people anciently, He pleads with you today:

"Come unto me, all ye that labour and are heavy laden, and I will give you rest.

"Take my yoke upon you, and learn of me; for I am meek and lowly in heart: and ye shall find rest unto your souls.

"For my yoke is easy, and my burden is light" (Matthew 11:28–30).

"Will ye not now return unto me, and repent of your sins, and be converted, that I may heal you?

"Yea, verily I say unto you, if ye will come unto me ye shall have eternal life. Behold, mine arm of mercy is extended towards you, and whosoever will come, him will I receive; and blessed are those who come unto me" (3 Nephi 9:13 14).

For an explanation of repentance, see "Repentance," pages 132–35.

## Forgiving Others

In addition to seeking forgiveness for our own sins, we must be willing to forgive others. The Lord said: "Ye ought to forgive one another; for he that forgiveth not his brother his trespasses standeth condemned before the Lord; for there remaineth in him the greater sin. I, the Lord, will forgive whom I will forgive, but of you it is required to forgive all men" (D&C 64:9–10).

In the everyday circumstances of life, you will surely be wronged by other people—sometimes innocently and sometimes intentionally. It is easy to become bitter or angry or vengeful in such situations, but this is not the Lord's way. The Savior counseled, "Love your enemies, bless them that curse you, do good to them that hate you, and pray for them which despitefully use you, and persecute you" (Matthew 5:44). He set the perfect example of forgiveness when He was on the cross. Referring to the Roman soldiers who had crucified Him, He prayed, "Father, forgive them; for they know not what they do" (Luke 23:34; see footnote *c*).

Pray for strength to forgive those who have wronged you. Abandon feelings of anger, bitterness, or revenge. Look for the good in others rather than focusing on their faults and magnifying their weaknesses. Allow God to be the judge of others' harmful actions. It may be difficult to let go of hurt feelings, but you can do it with the Lord's help. You will find that forgiveness can heal terrible wounds, replacing the poison of contention and hatred with the peace and love that only God can give.

Additional references: Matthew 6:14–15; 18:21–22; 1 Nephi 7:16–21

*See also* Atonement of Jesus Christ; Judging Others; Repentance

## Fornication (*See* Chastity)

## Gambling

The Church of Jesus Christ of Latter-day Saints is opposed to gambling, including lotteries sponsored by governments.

Gambling is motivated by a desire to get something for nothing. This desire is spiritually destructive. It leads participants away from the Savior's teachings of love and service and toward the selfishness of the adversary. It undermines the virtues of work and thrift and the desire to give honest effort in all we do.

Those who participate in gambling soon discover the deception in the idea that they can give little or nothing and receive something of value in return. They find that they give up large amounts of money, their own honor, and the respect of family members and friends. Deceived and addicted, they often gamble with funds they should use for other purposes, such as meeting the basic needs of their families. Gamblers sometimes become so enslaved and so desperate to pay gambling debts that they turn to stealing, giving up their own good name.

The First Presidency has encouraged us to join with others in opposing the legalization and government sponsorship of any form of gambling in our communities.

*See also* Temptation

**Garments** (*See* Temples)

**General Authorities** (*See* Church Administration)

**Gift of the Holy Ghost** (*See* Holy Ghost)

**Gifts of the Spirit** (*See* Spiritual Gifts)

## Godhead

The first article of faith states, "We believe in God, the Eternal Father, and in His Son, Jesus Christ, and in the Holy Ghost." These three beings make up the Godhead. They preside over this world and all other creations of our Father in Heaven.

The true doctrine of the Godhead was lost in the apostasy that followed the Savior's mortal ministry and the deaths of His Apostles. This doctrine began to be restored when 14-year-old Joseph Smith received his First Vision (see Joseph Smith—History 1:17). From the Prophet's account of the First Vision and from his other teachings, we know that the members of the Godhead are three separate beings. The Father and the Son have tangible bodies of flesh and bones, and the Holy Ghost is a personage of spirit (see D&C 130:22).

Although the members of the Godhead are distinct beings with distinct roles, they are one in purpose and doctrine. They are perfectly united in bringing to pass Heavenly Father's divine plan of salvation.

Additional references: Matthew 3:13–17; John 14:6–10; 17:6–23; Acts 7:55–56; 2 Nephi 31:18; Mormon 7:5–7; D&C 76:20–24

*See also* God the Father; Holy Ghost; Jesus Christ

## God the Father

God the Father is the Supreme Being in whom we believe and whom we worship. He is the ultimate Creator, Ruler, and Preserver of all things. He is perfect, has all power, and knows all things. He "has a body of flesh and bones as tangible as man's" (D&C 130:22).

Our Heavenly Father is a God of judgment and strength and knowledge and power, but He is also a God of perfect mercy, kindness, and charity. Even though we "do not know the meaning of all things," we can find peace in the sure knowledge that He loves us (see 1 Nephi 11:17).

### The Father of Our Spirits

One of life's great questions is "Who am I?" A beloved Primary song helps even little children answer this question. We sing, "I am a child of God, and he has sent me here." The knowledge that we are children of God provides strength, comfort, and hope.

You are a literal child of God, spiritually begotten in the premortal life. As His child, you can be assured that you have divine, eternal potential and that He will help you in your sincere efforts to reach that potential.

### The Supreme Creator

Heavenly Father is the Supreme Creator. Through Jesus Christ, He created heaven and earth and all things in them (see Moses 2:1). Alma said, "All things denote there is a God; yea, even the earth, and all things that are upon the face of it, yea, and its motion, yea, and also all the planets which move in their regular form do witness that there is a Supreme Creator" (Alma 30:44).

From time to time, ponder the beauties of creation: trees, flowers, animals, mountains, the waves of the ocean, a new-born child. Take time to gaze into the heavens, where the courses of the stars and planets are evidence of "God moving in his majesty and power" (see D&C 88:41–47).

## The Author of the Plan of Salvation

Our Father in Heaven wants us to dwell with Him eternally. His work and glory is "to bring to pass the immortality and eternal life of man" (Moses 1:39). In order to make this possible, He prepared the plan of salvation. He sent His Beloved Son, Jesus Christ, to loose the bands of death and atone for the sins of the world: "For God so loved the world, that he gave his only begotten Son, that whosoever believeth in him should not perish, but have everlasting life" (John 3:16). This sacrifice is the greatest expression of our Father's love for us.

## Coming to Know God the Father

As children of God, we have a special relationship with Him, setting us apart from all His other creations. Seek to know your Father in Heaven. He loves you, and He has given you the precious opportunity to draw near to Him as you pray. Your prayers, offered in humility and sincerity, are heard and answered.

You can also come to know your Father by learning about His Beloved Son and applying the gospel in your life. The Savior taught His disciples: "If ye had known me, ye should have known my Father also. . . . He that hath seen me hath seen the Father" (John 14:7, 9).

You draw near to God the Father as you study the scriptures and the words of latter-day prophets and as you give service. When you follow God's will and live as He would have you live, you become more like Him and His Son. You prepare yourself to return to live in Their presence.

Additional references: John 14:6, 21–24; 17:3; Mosiah 4:9; D&C 132:22–24; Articles of Faith 1:1

*See also* Creation; Godhead; Plan of Salvation

## Gospel

The gospel is our Heavenly Father's plan of happiness. The central doctrine of the gospel is the Atonement of Jesus Christ.

The Prophet Joseph Smith said, "The first principles and ordinances of the Gospel are: first, Faith in the Lord Jesus Christ; second, Repentance; third, Baptism by immersion for the remission of sins; fourth, Laying on of hands for the gift of the Holy Ghost" (Articles of Faith 1:4). In its fulness, the gospel includes all the doctrines, principles, laws, ordinances, and covenants necessary for us to be exalted in the celestial kingdom. The Savior has promised that if we endure to the end, faithfully living the gospel, He will hold us guiltless before the Father at the Final Judgment (see 3 Nephi 27:16).

The fulness of the gospel has been preached in all ages when God's children have been prepared to receive it. In the latter days, or the dispensation of the fulness of times, the gospel has been restored through the Prophet Joseph Smith.

Additional references: Romans 1:16–17; 3 Nephi 27:13–22; D&C 11:24; 39:5–6

*See also* Atonement of Jesus Christ; Baptism; Faith; Holy Ghost; Jesus Christ; Plan of Salvation; Repentance; Restoration of the Gospel

## Government (*See* Civil Government and Law)

## Grace

The word *grace,* as used in the scriptures, refers primarily to the divine help and strength we receive through the Atonement of the Lord Jesus Christ. The Apostle Peter taught that we should "grow in grace, and in the knowledge of our Lord and Saviour Jesus Christ" (2 Peter 3:18).

Salvation by Grace

Because of the Fall, everyone will experience temporal death. Through grace, made available by the Savior's atoning sacrifice, all people will be resurrected and receive immortality (see 2 Nephi 9:6–13). But resurrection alone does not qualify us for eternal life in the presence of God. Our sins make us unclean and unfit to dwell in God's presence, and we need His grace to purify and perfect us "after all we can do" (2 Nephi 25:23).

The phrase "after all we can do" teaches that effort is required on our part to receive the fulness of the Lord's grace and be made worthy to dwell with Him. The Lord has commanded us to obey His gospel, which includes having faith in Him, repenting of our sins, being baptized, receiving the gift of the Holy Ghost, and enduring to the end (see John 3:3–5; 3 Nephi 27:16–20; Articles of Faith 1:3–4). The prophet Moroni wrote of the grace we receive as we come unto the Savior and obey His teachings:

"Come unto Christ, and be perfected in him, and deny yourselves of all ungodliness; and if ye shall deny yourselves of all ungodliness, and love God with all your might, mind and strength, then is his grace sufficient for you, that by his grace ye may be perfect in Christ; and if by the grace of God ye are perfect in Christ, ye can in nowise deny the power of God.

"And again, if ye by the grace of God are perfect in Christ, and deny not his power, then are ye sanctified in Christ by the grace of God, through the shedding of the blood of Christ, which is in the covenant of the Father unto the remission of your sins, that ye become holy, without spot" (Moroni 10:32–33).

Receiving Grace throughout Your Life

In addition to needing grace for your ultimate salvation, you need this enabling power every day of your life. As you draw near to your Heavenly Father in diligence, humility, and meekness, He will uplift and strengthen you through His grace (see Proverbs 3:34; 1 Peter 5:5; D&C 88:78; 106:7–8). Reliance upon His grace enables you to progress and grow in righteousness. Jesus Himself "received not of the fulness at first, but continued from grace to grace, until he received a fulness" (D&C 93:13). Grace enables you to help build God's kingdom, a service you cannot give through your strength or means alone (see John 15:5; Philippians 4:13; Hebrews 12:28; Jacob 4:6–7).

If you ever become discouraged or feel too weak to continue living the gospel, remember the strength you can receive through the enabling power of grace. You can find comfort and assurance in these words of the Lord: "My grace is sufficient for all men that humble themselves before me; for if they humble themselves before me, and have faith in me, then will I make weak things become strong unto them" (Ether 12:27).

Additional references: Acts 15:11; Romans 5:2; 2 Nephi 10:24; 11:5

*See also* Atonement of Jesus Christ; Resurrection; Salvation

# Gratitude

The Lord has promised, "He who receiveth all things with thankfulness shall be made glorious" (D&C 78:19). Gratitude is an uplifting, exalting attitude. You can probably say from experience that you are happier when you have gratitude in your heart. You cannot be bitter, resentful, or mean-spirited when you are grateful.

Be thankful for the wonderful blessings that are yours. Be grateful for the tremendous opportunities you have. Be thankful to your parents. Let them know of your gratitude. Thank your friends and your teachers. Express appreciation to everyone who does you a favor or assists you in any way.

Thank your Heavenly Father for His goodness to you. You can express your gratitude to God by acknowledging His hand in all things, thanking Him for all that He gives you, keeping His commandments, and serving others. Thank Him for His Beloved Son, Jesus Christ. Express thanks for the Savior's great example, for His teachings, for His outreaching hand to lift and help, for His infinite Atonement.

Thank the Lord for His restored Church. Thank Him for all that it offers you. Thank Him for friends and family. Let a spirit of thanksgiving guide and bless your days and nights. Work at being grateful. You will find that it yields wonderful results.

Additional references: Psalm 100:3–4; Luke 17:11–19; Mosiah 2:19–22; Alma 34:38; D&C 59:7

## Happiness

Testifying of God's "eternal purposes," the prophet Lehi taught, "Men are, that they might have joy" (2 Nephi 2:15, 25).

Heavenly Father desires that we find true, lasting happiness. Our happiness is the design of all the blessings He gives us—gospel teachings, commandments, priesthood ordinances, family relationships, prophets, temples, the beauties of creation, and even the opportunity to experience adversity. His plan for our salvation is often called "the great plan of happiness" (Alma 42:8). He sent His Beloved Son to carry out the Atonement so we can be happy in this life and receive a fulness of joy in the eternities.

Many people try to find happiness and fulfillment in activities that are contrary to the Lord's commandments.

Ignoring God's plan for them, they reject the only source of real happiness. They give in to the devil, who "seeketh that all men might be miserable like unto himself" (2 Nephi 2:27). Eventually they learn the truth of Alma's warning to his son Corianton: "Wickedness never was happiness" (Alma 41:10).

Others seek only to have fun in life. With this as their main goal, they allow temporary pleasure to distract them from lasting happiness. They rob themselves of the enduring joys of spiritual growth, service, and hard work.

As you seek to be happy, remember that the only way to real happiness is to live the gospel. You will find peaceful, eternal happiness as you strive to keep the commandments, pray for strength, repent of your sins, participate in wholesome activities, and give meaningful service. You will learn to have fun within the limits set by a loving Father in Heaven.

Your happiness can be contagious. As others observe you, they may desire to know the source of your joy. Then they can also experience the happiness that comes through living the gospel of Jesus Christ.

Additional references: Psalm 35:9; 2 Nephi 5:27; Mosiah 2:41; 3 Nephi 17:18–20; 4 Nephi 1:15–16; D&C 18:10–16

*See also* Missionary Work; Plan of Salvation; Service

## Heaven

In the scriptures, the word *heaven* is used in two basic ways. First, it refers to the place where God lives, which is the ultimate home of the faithful (see Mosiah 2:41). Second, it refers to the expanse around the earth (see Genesis 1:1).

Additional references: Psalm 11:4; Matthew 6:9; 1 Nephi 1:8; Mosiah 3:8; D&C 20:17

*See also* Kingdoms of Glory

**Heavenly Father** (*See* God the Father)

# Hell

Latter-day revelations speak of hell in at least two ways. First, it is another name for spirit prison, a place in the post-mortal spirit world for those who have "died in their sins, without a knowledge of the truth, or in transgression, having rejected the prophets" (D&C 138:32). This is a temporary state in which spirits will be taught the gospel and have the opportunity to repent and accept ordinances of salvation that are performed for them in temples (see D&C 138:30–35). Those who accept the gospel may dwell in paradise until the Resurrection. After they are resurrected and judged, they will receive the degree of glory of which they are worthy. Those who choose not to repent but who are not sons of perdition will remain in spirit prison until the end of the Millennium, when they will be freed from hell and punishment and be resurrected to a telestial glory (see D&C 76:81–85).

Second, the word *hell* is used to refer to outer darkness, which is the dwelling place of the devil, his angels, and the sons of perdition (see D&C 29:36–38; 76:28–33). Sons of perdition are those who receive "no forgiveness in this world nor in the world to come—having denied the Holy Spirit after having received it, and having denied the Only Begotten Son of the Father, having crucified him unto themselves and put him to an open shame" (D&C 76:34–35; see also verses 31–33, 36–37). Such individuals will not inherit a place in any kingdom of glory; for them the conditions of hell remain (see D&C 76:38; 88:24, 32).

*See also* Kingdoms of Glory; Satan

# Holy Ghost

The Holy Ghost is the third member of the Godhead. He is a personage of spirit, without a body of flesh and bones (see D&C 130:22). He is often referred to as the Spirit, the

Holy Spirit, the Spirit of God, the Spirit of the Lord, or the Comforter.

Roles of the Holy Ghost

The Holy Ghost works in perfect unity with Heavenly Father and Jesus Christ, fulfilling several roles to help you live righteously and receive the blessings of the gospel.

He "witnesses of the Father and the Son" (2 Nephi 31:18) and reveals and teaches "the truth of all things" (Moroni 10:5). You can receive a sure testimony of Heavenly Father and Jesus Christ only by the power of the Holy Ghost. His communication to your spirit carries far more certainty than any communication you can receive through your natural senses.

As you strive to stay on the path that leads to eternal life, the Holy Ghost "will show unto you all things what [you] should do" (see 2 Nephi 32:1–5). He can guide you in your decisions and protect you from physical and spiritual danger.

Through Him, you can receive gifts of the Spirit for your benefit and for the benefit of those you love and serve (see D&C 46:9–11).

He is the Comforter (John 14:26). As the soothing voice of a loving parent can quiet a crying child, the whisperings of the Spirit can calm your fears, hush the nagging worries of your life, and comfort you when you grieve. The Holy Ghost can fill you "with hope and perfect love" and "teach you the peaceable things of the kingdom" (Moroni 8:26; D&C 36:2).

Through His power, you are sanctified as you repent, receive the ordinances of baptism and confirmation, and remain true to your covenants (see Mosiah 5:1–6; 3 Nephi 27:20; Moses 6:64–68).

He is the Holy Spirit of Promise (see Ephesians 1:13; D&C 132:7, 18–19, 26). In this capacity, He confirms that the priesthood ordinances you have received and the covenants you have made are acceptable to God. This approval depends on your continued faithfulness.

The Gift of the Holy Ghost

All honest seekers of the truth can feel the influence of the Holy Ghost, leading them to Jesus Christ and His gospel. However, the fulness of the blessings given through the Holy Ghost are available only to those who receive the gift of the Holy Ghost and remain worthy.

After you were baptized into The Church of Jesus Christ of Latter-day Saints, one or more Melchizedek Priesthood holders laid their hands on your head and, in a sacred priesthood ordinance, confirmed you a member of the Church. As part of this ordinance, called confirmation, you were given the gift of the Holy Ghost.

The gift of the Holy Ghost is different from the influence of the Holy Ghost. Before your baptism, you could feel the influence of the Holy Ghost from time to time, and through that influence you could receive a testimony of the truth. Now that you have the gift of the Holy Ghost, you have the right to the constant companionship of that member of the Godhead if you keep the commandments.

Full enjoyment of the gift of the Holy Ghost includes receiving revelation and comfort, serving and blessing others through spiritual gifts, and being sanctified from sin and made fit for exaltation in the celestial kingdom. These blessings depend on your worthiness; they come a little at a time as you are ready for them. As you bring your life in harmony with God's will, you gradually receive the Holy Ghost in great measure. The Prophet Joseph Smith declared that the mysteries of God's kingdom "are only to be seen and understood by the power of the Holy Spirit, which God bestows on those who love him, and purify themselves before him" (see D&C 76:114–116).

Remember that "the Spirit of the Lord doth not dwell in unholy temples" (Helaman 4:24). Even though you have received the gift of the Holy Ghost, the Spirit will dwell with you only when you keep the commandments. He will

withdraw if you offend Him by profanity, uncleanliness, disobedience, rebellion, or other sins. Keep yourself clean. Fill
your life with goodness so you can be worthy of the constant
companionship of the Holy Ghost.

Additional references: Matthew 3:11; John 15:26; 16:13; Acts 2:38; 8:12–17;
19:1–6; 1 Corinthians 2:9–14; 12:3; Galatians 5:22–23; 1 Nephi 10:17–19; 2
Nephi 31:17; D&C 8:2–3; 39:20–24; 68:25–28; 121:46; Articles of Faith 1:4

*See also* Baptism; Godhead; Laying On of Hands; Revelation; Spiritual Gifts

## Home Teaching *(See* Priesthood)

## Homosexuality *(See* Chastity)

## Honesty

The thirteenth article of faith states, "We believe in being
honest." To be honest means to be sincere, truthful, and without deceit at all times.

When you are honest in every way, you are able to enjoy
peace of mind and maintain self-respect. You build strength
of character, which allows you to be of service to God and others. You are trustworthy in the eyes of God and those around
you.

On the other hand, if you are dishonest in your words
or actions, you hurt yourself and often hurt others as well.
If you lie, steal, cheat, or neglect to give the full amount of
work for your pay, you lose your self-respect. You lose the
guidance of the Holy Ghost. You may find that you have
damaged relationships with family members and friends and
that people no longer trust you.

Being honest often requires courage and sacrifice, especially when others try to persuade you to justify dishonest
behavior. If you find yourself in such a situation, remember
that the lasting peace that comes from being honest is more
valuable than the momentary relief of following the crowd.

Additional references: Exodus 20:16; 2 Nephi 9:34; D&C 97:8

## Hope

The word *hope* is sometimes misunderstood. In our everyday language, the word often has a hint of uncertainty. For example, we may say that we hope for a change in the weather or a visit from a friend. In the language of the gospel, however, the word *hope* is sure, unwavering, and active. Prophets speak of having a "firm hope" (Alma 34:41) and a "lively hope" (1 Peter 1:3). The prophet Moroni taught, "Whoso believeth in God might with surety hope for a better world, yea, even a place at the right hand of God, which hope cometh of faith, maketh an anchor to the souls of men, which would make them sure and steadfast, always abounding in good works, being led to glorify God" (Ether 12:4).

When we have hope, we trust God's promises. We have a quiet assurance that if we do "the works of righteousness," we "shall receive [our] reward, even peace in this world, and eternal life in the world to come" (D&C 59:23). Mormon taught that such hope comes only through the Atonement of Jesus Christ: "What is it that ye shall hope for? Behold I say unto you that ye shall have hope through the atonement of Christ and the power of his resurrection, to be raised unto life eternal, and this because of your faith in him according to the promise" (Moroni 7:41).

As you strive to live the gospel, you grow in your ability to "abound in hope, through the power of the Holy Ghost" (Romans 15:13). You increase in hope as you pray and seek God's forgiveness. In the Book of Mormon, a missionary named Aaron assured a Lamanite king, "If thou wilt repent of all thy sins, and will bow down before God, and call on his name in faith, believing that ye shall receive, then shalt thou receive the hope which thou desirest" (Alma 22:16). You also gain hope as you study the scriptures and follow their teachings. The Apostle Paul taught, "Whatsoever things were written aforetime were written for our learning, that we through patience and comfort of the scriptures might have hope" (Romans 15:4).

The principle of hope extends into the eternities, but it also can sustain you through the everyday challenges of life. "Happy is he," said the Psalmist, "that hath the God of Jacob for his help, whose hope is in the Lord his God" (Psalm 146:5). With hope, you can find joy in life. You can "have patience, and bear with . . . afflictions, with a firm hope that ye shall one day rest from all your afflictions" (Alma 34:41). You can "press forward with a steadfastness in Christ, having a perfect brightness of hope, and a love of God and of all men. Wherefore, if ye shall press forward, feasting upon the word of Christ, and endure to the end, behold, thus saith the Father: Ye shall have eternal life" (2 Nephi 31:20).

Additional references: Lamentations 3:25–26; 1 Corinthians 15:19–22; 1 Peter 3:15; 1 John 3:2–3; Jacob 4:4–6; Alma 13:28–29; 27:28; Ether 12:32; Moroni 8:26; 9:25; 10:22

*See also* Adversity; Atonement of Jesus Christ; Charity; Faith

**Hot Drinks** (*See* Word of Wisdom)

## Humility

To be humble is to recognize gratefully your dependence on the Lord—to understand that you have constant need for His support. Humility is an acknowledgment that your talents and abilities are gifts from God. It is not a sign of weakness, timidity, or fear; it is an indication that you know where your true strength lies. You can be both humble and fearless. You can be both humble and courageous.

Jesus Christ is our greatest example of humility. During His mortal ministry, He always acknowledged that His strength came because of His dependence on His Father. He said: "I can of mine own self do nothing. . . . I seek not mine own will, but the will of the Father which hath sent me" (John 5:30).

The Lord will strengthen you as you humble yourself before Him. James taught: "God resistéth the proud, but giveth grace unto the humble. . . . Humble yourselves in the sight of the Lord, and he shall lift you up" (James 4:6, 10).

Additional references: Matthew 18:4; 23:12; 26:39; Luke 22:42; 1 Peter 5:5–6; Mosiah 4:11–12; 15:6–7; Alma 5:27–28; Helaman 3:33–35; Ether 12:27; D&C 12:8; 67:10; 112:10; 136:32–33

## Jesus Christ

On January 1, 2000, the First Presidency and Quorum of the Twelve Apostles issued the following declaration. Titled "The Living Christ," this declaration bears witness of the Lord Jesus Christ and summarizes His identity and divine mission:

"As we commemorate the birth of Jesus Christ two millennia ago, we offer our testimony of the reality of His matchless life and the infinite virtue of His great atoning sacrifice. None other has had so profound an influence upon all who have lived and will yet live upon the earth.

"He was the Great Jehovah of the Old Testament, the Messiah of the New. Under the direction of His Father, He was the creator of the earth. 'All things were made by him; and without him was not any thing made that was made' (John 1:3). Though sinless, He was baptized to fulfill all righteousness. He 'went about doing good' (Acts 10:38), yet was despised for it. His gospel was a message of peace and goodwill. He entreated all to follow His example. He walked the roads of Palestine, healing the sick, causing the blind to see, and raising the dead. He taught the truths of eternity, the reality of our premortal existence, the purpose of our life on earth, and the potential for the sons and daughters of God in the life to come.

"He instituted the sacrament as a reminder of His great atoning sacrifice. He was arrested and condemned on spurious charges, convicted to satisfy a mob, and sentenced to die on Calvary's cross. He gave His life to atone for the sins of all mankind. His was a great vicarious gift in behalf of all who would ever live upon the earth.

"We solemnly testify that His life, which is central to all human history, neither began in Bethlehem nor concluded on Calvary. He was the Firstborn of the Father, the Only Begotten Son in the flesh, the Redeemer of the world.

"He rose from the grave to 'become the firstfruits of them that slept' (1 Corinthians 15:20). As Risen Lord, He visited among those He had loved in life. He also ministered among His 'other sheep' (John 10:16) in ancient America. In the modern world, He and His Father appeared to the boy Joseph Smith, ushering in the long-promised 'dispensation of the fulness of times' (Ephesians 1:10).

"Of the Living Christ, the Prophet Joseph wrote: 'His eyes were as a flame of fire; the hair of his head was white like the pure snow; his countenance shone above the brightness of the sun; and his voice was as the sound of the rushing of great waters, even the voice of Jehovah, saying:

" 'I am the first and the last; I am he who liveth, I am he who was slain; I am your advocate with the Father' (D&C 110:3–4).

"Of Him the Prophet also declared: 'And now, after the many testimonies which have been given of him, this is the testimony, last of all, which we give of him: That he lives!

" 'For we saw him, even on the right hand of God; and we heard the voice bearing record that he is the Only Begotten of the Father—

" 'That by him, and through him, and of him, the worlds are and were created, and the inhabitants thereof are begotten sons and daughters unto God' (D&C 76:22–24).

"We declare in words of solemnity that His priesthood and His Church have been restored upon the earth—'built upon the foundation of . . . apostles and prophets, Jesus Christ himself being the chief corner stone' (Ephesians 2:20).

"We testify that He will someday return to earth. 'And the glory of the Lord shall be revealed, and all flesh shall see it together' (Isaiah 40:5). He will rule as King of Kings and reign as Lord of Lords, and every knee shall bend and every tongue shall speak in worship before Him. Each of us will stand to be judged of Him according to our works and the desires of our hearts.

"We bear testimony, as His duly ordained Apostles—that Jesus is the Living Christ, the immortal Son of God. He is the great King Immanuel, who stands today on the right hand of His Father. He is the light, the life, and the hope of the world. His way is the path that leads to happiness in this life and eternal life in the world to come. God be thanked for the matchless gift of His divine Son" (*Ensign,* Apr. 2000, 2–3).

*See also* Atonement of Jesus Christ

## Joseph Smith

In the spring of 1820, 14-year-old Joseph Smith was searching for the true Church of Jesus Christ when he read a passage in the Bible: "If any of you lack wisdom, let him ask of God, that giveth to all men liberally, and upbraideth not; and it shall be given him" (James 1:5; see also Joseph Smith—History 1:11–12). With simple, unwavering faith, young Joseph followed the counsel in that passage. He went alone to a grove of trees, where he prayed to know which church he should join. In answer to his prayer, God the Father and Jesus Christ appeared to him. Among other things, They told him that he should join none of the churches then in existence. (See Joseph Smith—History 1:13–20.)

As Joseph Smith proved his worthiness, he was given a divine mission as a prophet of God. Through him, the Lord accomplished a great and marvelous work that included bringing forth the Book of Mormon, restoring the priesthood, revealing precious gospel truths, organizing the true Church of Jesus Christ, and establishing temple work. On June 27, 1844, Joseph and his brother Hyrum were killed in an attack by an armed mob. They sealed their testimonies with their blood.

For your testimony of the restored gospel to be complete, it must include a testimony of Joseph Smith's divine mission. The truthfulness of The Church of Jesus Christ of Latter-day Saints rests on the truthfulness of the First Vision and the other revelations the Lord gave to the Prophet Joseph. President John Taylor, the third President of the Church, wrote, "Joseph Smith, the Prophet and Seer of the Lord, has done more, save Jesus only, for the salvation of men in this world, than any other man that ever lived in it" (D&C 135:3).

Additional references: Isaiah 29:13–14; 2 Nephi 3:3–15; D&C 5:9–10; 135; Joseph Smith—History

*See also* Prophets; Restoration of the Gospel

## Judging Others

Sometimes people feel that it is wrong to judge others in any way. While it is true that you should not condemn others or judge them unrighteously, you will need to make judgments of ideas, situations, and people throughout your life. The Lord has given many commandments that you cannot keep without making judgments. For example, He has said: "Beware of false prophets. . . . Ye shall know them by their fruits" (Matthew 7:15–16) and "Go ye out from among the wicked" (D&C 38:42). You need to make judgments of people in many of your important decisions, such as choosing friends, voting for government leaders, and choosing an eternal companion.

Judgment is an important use of your agency and requires great care, especially when you make judgments about other people. All your judgments must be guided by righteous standards. Remember that only God, who knows each individual's heart, can make final judgments of individuals (see Revelation 20:12; 3 Nephi 27:14; D&C 137:9).

The Lord gave a warning to guide us in our judgment of others: "With what judgment ye judge, ye shall be judged; and with what measure ye mete, it shall be measured to you again. And why beholdest thou the mote that is in thy brother's eye, but considerest not the beam that is in thine own eye? Or how wilt thou say to thy brother: Let me pull the mote out of thine eye—and behold, a beam is in thine own eye? Thou hypocrite, first cast the beam out of thine own eye; and then shalt thou see clearly to cast the mote out of thy brother's eye" (3 Nephi 14:2–5).

In this scripture passage the Lord teaches that a fault we see in another is often like a tiny speck in that person's eye, compared to our own faults, which are like an enormous beam in our eyes. Sometimes we focus on others' faults when we should instead be working to improve ourselves.

Your righteous judgments about others can provide needed guidance for them and, in some cases, protection for you and your family. Approach any such judgment with care and compassion. As much as you can, judge people's situations rather than judging the people themselves. Whenever possible, refrain from making judgments until you have an adequate knowledge of the facts. Always be sensitive to the Holy Spirit, who can guide your decisions. Remember Alma's counsel to his son Corianton: "See that you are merciful unto your brethren; deal justly, judge righteously, and do good continually" (Alma 41:14).

Additional references: 1 Samuel 16:7; Moroni 7:14–19; D&C 11:12

*See also* Charity; Forgiveness; Love; Mercy

## Justice

Justice is the unchanging law that brings consequences for actions. Because of the law of justice, you receive blessings when you obey God's commandments (see D&C 130:21–22). The law of justice also demands that a penalty be paid for every sin you commit. It requires that no unclean thing be permitted to dwell with God (see 1 Nephi 10:21).

When the Savior carried out the Atonement, He took our sins upon Himself. He was able to "answer the ends of the law" (2 Nephi 2:7) because He subjected Himself to the penalty that the law required for our sins. In doing so, He "satisfied the demands of justice" and extended mercy to everyone who repents and follows Him (see Mosiah 15:9; Alma 34:14–16). Because He has paid the price for your sins, you will not have to suffer that punishment if you repent (see D&C 19:15–20).

Additional references: 2 Nephi 9:26; Alma 42

*See also* Atonement of Jesus Christ; Mercy; Repentance

## Keys of the Priesthood (*See* Priesthood)

## Kingdoms of Glory

Through the Atonement of Jesus Christ, all people will be resurrected (see Alma 11:42–45). After we are resurrected, we will stand before the Lord to be judged (see Revelation 20:12; 3 Nephi 27:14). Each of us will be assigned to an eternal dwelling place in a specific kingdom of glory. The Lord taught this principle when He said, "In my Father's house are many mansions" (John 14:2).

There are three kingdoms of glory: the celestial kingdom, the terrestrial kingdom, and the telestial kingdom. The glory you inherit will depend on the depth of your conversion, expressed by your obedience to the Lord's commandments. It will depend on the manner in which you have "received the testimony of Jesus" (D&C 76:51; see also verses 74, 79, 101).

### Celestial Kingdom

The celestial kingdom is the highest of the three kingdoms of glory. Those in this kingdom will dwell forever in the presence of God the Father and His Son Jesus Christ. This should be your goal: to inherit celestial glory and to help others receive that great blessing as well. Such a goal is not achieved in one attempt; it is the result of a lifetime of righteousness and constancy of purpose.

The celestial kingdom is the place prepared for those who have "received the testimony of Jesus" and been "made perfect through Jesus the mediator of the new covenant, who wrought out this perfect atonement through the shedding of his own blood" (D&C 76:51, 69). To inherit this gift, we must receive the ordinances of salvation, keep the commandments, and repent of our sins. For a detailed explanation of those who will inherit celestial glory, see Doctrine and Covenants 76:50–70, 92–96.

In January 1836 the Prophet Joseph Smith received a revelation that expanded his understanding of the requirements to inherit celestial glory. The heavens were opened to him, and he saw the celestial kingdom. He marveled when he saw his older brother Alvin there, even though Alvin had died before receiving the ordinance of baptism. (See D&C 137:1–6.) Then the voice of the Lord came to the Prophet Joseph:

"All who have died without a knowledge of this gospel, who would have received it if they had been permitted to tarry, shall be heirs of the celestial kingdom of God;

"Also all that shall die henceforth without a knowledge of it, who would have received it with all their hearts, shall be heirs of that kingdom;

"For I, the Lord, will judge all men according to their works, according to the desire of their hearts" (D&C 137:7–9).

Commenting on this revelation, the Prophet Joseph said, "I also beheld that all children who die before they arrive at the years of accountability are saved in the celestial kingdom of heaven" (D&C 137:10).

From another revelation to the Prophet Joseph, we learn that there are three degrees within the celestial kingdom. To be exalted in the highest degree and continue eternally in family relationships, we must enter into "the new and everlasting covenant of marriage" and be true to that covenant. In other words, temple marriage is a requirement for obtaining the highest degree of celestial glory. (See D&C 131:1–4.) All who are worthy to enter into the new and everlasting covenant of marriage will have that opportunity, whether in this life or the next.

## Terrestrial Kingdom

Those who inherit terrestrial glory will "receive of the presence of the Son, but not of the fulness of the Father. Wherefore, they are bodies terrestrial, and not bodies celestial, and differ in glory as the moon differs from the sun" (D&C 76:77–78). Generally speaking, individuals in the terrestrial kingdom will be honorable people "who were blinded by the craftiness of men" (D&C 76:75). This group will include members of the Church who were "not valiant in the testimony of Jesus" (D&C 76:79). It will also include those who rejected the opportunity to receive the gospel in mortality but who later received it in the postmortal spirit world (see D&C 76:73–74). To learn more about those who will inherit terrestrial glory, see Doctrine and Covenants 76:71–80, 91, 97.

## Telestial Kingdom

Telestial glory will be reserved for individuals who "received not the gospel of Christ, neither the testimony of Jesus" (D&C 76:82). These individuals will receive their glory after being redeemed from spirit prison, which is sometimes called hell (see D&C 76:84, 106). A detailed explanation of those who will inherit telestial glory is found in Doctrine and Covenants 76:81–90, 98–106, 109–112.

## Perdition

Some people will not be worthy to dwell in any kingdom of glory. They will be called "the sons of perdition" and will have to "abide a kingdom which is not a kingdom of glory" (D&C 76:32; 88:24). This will be the state of "those who know [God's] power, and have been made partakers thereof, and suffered themselves through the power of the devil to be overcome, and to deny the truth and defy [God's] power" (D&C 76:31; see also verses 30, 32–49).

Additional references: 1 Corinthians 15:40–42, including footnote 40*a;* D&C 88:20–39; 130:18–19

*See also* Atonement of Jesus Christ; Eternal Life; Heaven; Hell; Plan of Salvation

## Laying On of Hands

The laying on of hands is the procedure revealed by the Lord for performing many priesthood ordinances, such as confirmation, ordination, setting members apart to serve in callings, administering to the sick, and giving other priesthood blessings (see D&C 42:44; Articles of Faith 1:4–5). Those having the proper priesthood authority place their hands upon the head of the person receiving the ordinance. In doing so, they serve as instruments through whom the Lord blesses His children (see D&C 36:2).

This procedure has always been used by priesthood holders. Adam ordained his righteous male descendants by the laying on of hands (see D&C 107:40–50). When Jacob pronounced blessings on Ephraim and Manasseh, he laid his hands on their heads (see Genesis 48:14–19). Alma "ordained priests and elders, by laying on his hands according to the order of God" (Alma 6:1). The Apostles Peter and John bestowed the gift of the Holy Ghost by the laying on of hands (see Acts 8:14–17). In this dispensation, John the Baptist conferred the Aaronic Priesthood upon Joseph Smith and Oliver Cowdery by the laying on of hands (see Joseph Smith— History 1:68–69).

Additional references: Numbers 27:18–23; Acts 19:1–6; 1 Timothy 4:14; D&C 33:15; 35:6

*See also* Holy Ghost; Priesthood

## Light of Christ

The Light of Christ "proceedeth forth from the presence of God to fill the immensity of space." It is "the light which is in all things, which giveth life to all things, which is the law by which all things are governed" (D&C 88:12–13; see also verses 6–11). This power is an influence for good in the lives of all people (see John 1:9; D&C 93:2). In the scriptures, the Light of Christ is sometimes called the Spirit of the Lord, the Spirit of God, the Spirit of Christ, or the Light of Life.

The Light of Christ should not be confused with the Holy Ghost. It is not a personage, as the Holy Ghost is. Its influence leads people to find the true gospel, be baptized, and receive the gift of the Holy Ghost (see John 12:46; Alma 26:14–15).

Conscience is a manifestation of the Light of Christ, enabling us to judge good from evil. The prophet Mormon taught: "The Spirit of Christ is given to every man, that he may know good from evil; wherefore, I show unto you the way to judge; for every thing which inviteth to do good, and to persuade to believe in Christ, is sent forth by the power and gift of Christ; wherefore ye may know with a perfect knowledge it is of God. . . . And now, my brethren, seeing that ye know the light by which ye may judge, which light is the light of Christ, see that ye do not judge wrongfully; for with that same judgment which ye judge ye shall also be judged" (Moroni 7:16, 18).

Additional references: John 8:12; Alma 28:14

*See also* Conscience; Holy Ghost

## Love

Love is a feeling of deep devotion, concern, and affection. Love for God and fellow men is a characteristic of disciples of Jesus Christ (see Matthew 22:35–40; John 13:34–35;

2 Nephi 31:20). We manifest our love for Heavenly Father by keeping His commandments and serving His children. Our expressions of love for others may include being kind to them, listening to them, mourning with them, comforting them, serving them, praying for them, sharing the gospel with them, and being their friend.

Our love for those around us increases when we remember that we are all children of God—that we are spirit brothers and sisters. The love that results from this realization has the power to transcend all boundaries of nation, creed, and color.

Additional references: Leviticus 19:18, 34; Deuteronomy 6:5; Luke 6:31–36; John 15:9–15; 1 John 4:7–21, including footnote 12*a*; Mosiah 4:14–15; D&C 4:5; 12:8; 112:11; 121:41–45

*See also* Charity; Mercy; Obedience; Service

## Marriage

In the world today, many people dismiss and even mock marriage and the family. Amid such confusing and destructive voices, the First Presidency and Quorum of the Twelve Apostles provide the consistent voice of truth. They "solemnly proclaim that marriage between a man and a woman is ordained of God and that the family is central to the Creator's plan for the eternal destiny of His children" (see "The Family: A Proclamation to the World," page 59 in this book).

Life's greatest joys are found in the family. Strong family relationships require effort, but such effort brings great happiness in this life and throughout eternity. Even if you have not had a happy family life in the past, you can seek to have a happy, eternal marriage and a loving relationship with family members.

The New and Everlasting Covenant of Marriage

In our Heavenly Father's plan of happiness, a man and a woman can be sealed to one another for time and all eternity. Those who are sealed in the temple have the assurance that their relationship will continue forever if they are true to their covenants. They know that nothing, not even death, can permanently separate them.

The covenant of eternal marriage is necessary for exaltation. The Lord revealed through Joseph Smith: "In the celestial glory there are three heavens or degrees; and in order to obtain the highest, a man must enter into this order of the priesthood [meaning the new and everlasting covenant of marriage]; and if he does not, he cannot obtain it. He may enter into the other, but that is the end of his kingdom; he cannot have an increase" (D&C 131:1–4).

After receiving the sealing ordinance and making sacred covenants in the temple, a couple must continue in faithfulness in order to receive the blessings of eternal marriage and exaltation. The Lord said:

"If a man marry a wife by my word, which is my law, and by the new and everlasting covenant, and it is sealed unto them by the Holy Spirit of promise, by him who is anointed, unto whom I have appointed this power and the keys of this priesthood; . . . and if [they] abide in my covenant, . . . it shall be done unto them in all things whatsoever my servant hath put upon them, in time, and through all eternity; and shall be of full force when they are out of the world" (D&C 132:19; for an explanation of the Holy Spirit of Promise, see page 82).

Preparing for Marriage

If you are single, prepare yourself carefully for marriage. Remember that there is no substitute for marrying in the temple. Prepare to marry the right person in the right place at the right time. Live worthy now of the kind of person you hope to marry.

Date only those who have high standards and in whose company you can maintain your high standards. Carefully plan positive and constructive activities so that you and your date are not left alone without anything to do. Stay in areas of safety where you can easily control yourself. Do not participate in conversations or activities that arouse sexual feelings.

Look for a companion of your own faith. Look for someone you can always honor and respect, someone who will complement you in your life. Before you marry, be sure you have found someone to whom you can give your entire heart, your entire love, your entire allegiance, your entire loyalty.

## Counsel for Those Who Do Not Marry

Some members of the Church remain single through no fault of their own, even though they want to marry. If you find yourself in this situation, be assured that "all things work together for good to them that love God" (Romans 8:28). As you remain worthy, you will someday, in this life or the next, be given all the blessings of an eternal family relationship. The Lord has made this promise repeatedly through His latter-day prophets.

If you are single and desire to be married, do not give up hope. At the same time, do not allow yourself to become preoccupied with your goal. Instead, become anxiously engaged in worthwhile activities. Look for ways to serve in your extended family and in your community. Accept and magnify Church callings. Keep yourself clean, both physically and spiritually. Continue to learn and develop and progress in your personal life.

## Achieving a Happy Marriage

If you are married, remember that the friendship and love between you and your spouse should be your most cherished earthly relationship. Your spouse is the only person other than the Lord whom you have been commanded to love with all your heart (see D&C 42:22).

Remember that marriage, in its truest sense, is a partnership of equals, with neither person exercising dominion over the other, but with each encouraging, comforting, and helping the other.

Because marriage is such an important relationship in life, it needs and deserves time. Do not give higher priority to less-important commitments. Take time to talk together and to listen to one another. Be thoughtful and respectful. Express tender feelings and affection often.

Determine that nothing will ever come between you and your spouse to disrupt your marriage. Resolve to make your marriage succeed, in spite of challenges that may arise.

Be loyal to one another. Be faithful in your marriage covenants in thought, word, and deed. Remember that the Lord has said, "Thou shalt love thy wife with all thy heart, and shalt cleave unto her and none else" (D&C 42:22). The phrase "none else" teaches that no person, activity, or possession should ever take precedence over your relationship with your spouse.

Stay away from anything that could lead you to be unfaithful in any way. Pornography, unwholesome fantasies, and flirtations will erode your character and strike at the foundation of your marriage.

Work together to manage your finances. Cooperate in establishing and following a budget. Discipline yourselves in your spending, and avoid the bondage of debt. Wise money management and freedom from debt contribute to peace in the home.

Center your lives in the gospel of Jesus Christ. Help one another keep the covenants you have made. Attend church and the temple together. Study the scriptures together. Kneel together in prayer at the beginning and end of each day to thank your Heavenly Father for one another and to unite in asking for His blessings on your lives, your home, your loved ones, and your righteous desires. God will then guide you, and your daily conversations with Him will bring the peace and joy that can come from no other source. Your companionship will sweeten through the years; your love will strengthen. Your appreciation for one another will grow.

Additional references: Genesis 1:27–28; 2:18, 21–24; 1 Corinthians 11:11; Ephesians 5:22–33; Moses 2:27–28; 3:18, 21–24

*See also* Chastity; Divorce; Family; Temples; Unity

## Melchizedek Priesthood

"There are, in the church, two priesthoods, namely, the Melchizedek and Aaronic" (D&C 107:1). The Melchizedek Priesthood, which is "after the Order of the Son of God" (D&C 107:3), is the greater of these. It "holds the right of presidency, and has power and authority over all the offices in the church" (D&C 107:8). It also holds "the keys of all the spiritual blessings of the church" (D&C 107:18). It is named after a great high priest who lived during the time of the prophet Abraham (see D&C 107:2–4; see also Alma 13:14–19).

Through the authority of the Melchizedek Priesthood, Church leaders guide the Church and direct the preaching of the gospel throughout the world. In the ordinances of the Melchizedek Priesthood, "the power of godliness is manifest" (D&C 84:20).

This greater priesthood was given to Adam and has been on the earth whenever the Lord has revealed His gospel. It was taken from the earth during the Great Apostasy, but it was restored in May 1829, when the Apostles Peter, James, and John conferred it upon Joseph Smith and Oliver Cowdery.

The offices of the Melchizedek Priesthood are Apostle, Seventy, patriarch, high priest, and elder. The President of the High Priesthood is the President of the Church (see D&C 107:64–66).

Men in the Church must be worthy Melchizedek Priesthood holders in order to receive the temple endowment and be sealed to their families for eternity. They have the authority to administer to the sick and give special blessings to family members and others. With the authorization of presiding priesthood leaders, they can bestow the gift of the Holy Ghost and ordain other worthy men to offices in the Aaronic and Melchizedek Priesthoods.

When a man receives the Melchizedek Priesthood, he enters into the oath and covenant of the priesthood. He covenants to be faithful, magnify his calling, "give diligent heed to the words of eternal life," and "live by every word that proceedeth forth from the mouth of God." Those who keep this covenant will be sanctified by the Spirit and receive "all that [the] Father hath." (See D&C 84:33–44.)

*See also* Aaronic Priesthood; Priesthood

## Mercy

Our Heavenly Father knows our weaknesses and sins. He shows mercy when He forgives us of our sins and helps us return to dwell in His presence.

Such compassion may seem to conflict with the law of justice, which requires that no unclean thing be permitted to dwell with God (see 1 Nephi 10:21). But the Atonement of Jesus Christ made it possible for God to "be a perfect, just God, and a merciful God also" (Alma 42:15).

### Receiving God's Mercy

The Savior satisfied the demands of justice when He stood in our place and suffered the penalty for our sins. Because of this selfless act, the Father can mercifully withhold punishment from us and welcome us into His presence. To receive the Lord's forgiveness, we must sincerely repent of our sins. As the prophet Alma taught, "Justice exerciseth all his demands, and also mercy claimeth all which is her own; and thus, none but the truly penitent are saved" (Alma 42:24; see also verses 22–23, 25).

Forgiveness of sin is not the only gift of mercy from Heavenly Father and Jesus Christ. Every blessing you receive is an act of mercy, more than you could ever merit on your own. Mormon taught, "All things which are good cometh of Christ; otherwise men were fallen, and there could no good thing come unto them" (Moroni 7:24). For example, you are a recipient of divine mercy when Heavenly Father hears and answers your prayers, when you receive guidance from the Holy Ghost, and when you are healed from sickness through priesthood power. Although all such blessings come as results of your obedience, you could never receive them through your efforts alone. They are merciful gifts from a loving and compassionate Father.

### Showing Mercy for Others

Speaking to His disciples, the Savior commanded: "Be ye . . . merciful, as your Father also is merciful" (Luke 6:36) You can follow your Heavenly Father's example of mercy in your relationships with others. Strive to rid your life of arrogance, pride, and conceit. Seek ways to be compassionate, respectful, forgiving, gentle, and patient, even when you are aware of others' shortcomings. As you do so, your example will lead others to be more merciful, and you will have greater claim on the mercy of God.

Additional references: Matthew 5:7; Luke 10:25–37; Alma 34:14–16

*See also* Charity; Forgiveness; Grace; Justice

## Millennium

A millennium is a period of 1,000 years. When we speak of "the Millennium," we refer to the 1,000 years following the Savior's Second Coming (see Revelation 20:4; D&C 29:11).

During the Millennium, "Christ will reign personally upon the earth" (Articles of Faith 1:10).

The Millennium will be a time of righteousness and peace on the earth. The Lord has revealed that "in that day the enmity of man, and the enmity of beasts, yea, the enmity of all flesh, shall cease" (D&C 101:26; see also Isaiah 11:6–9). Satan will be "bound, that he shall have no place in the hearts of the children of men" (D&C 45:55; see also Revelation 20:1–3).

During the Millennium, all people on the earth will be good and just, but many will not have received the fulness of the gospel. Consequently, members of the Church will participate in missionary work.

Members of the Church will also participate in temple work during the Millennium. The Saints will continue to build temples and receive ordinances in behalf of their kindred dead. Guided by revelation, they will prepare records of their ancestors all the way back to Adam and Eve.

Complete righteousness and peace will continue until the end of the 1,000 years, when Satan "shall be loosed for a little season, that he may gather together his armies." The armies of Satan will fight against the hosts of heaven, who will be led by Michael, or Adam. Satan and his followers will be defeated and cast out forever. (See D&C 88:111–115.)

Additional references: D&C 45:55–59; 101:22–34; 133:25

*See also* Second Coming of Jesus Christ

## Missionary Work

When we experience the blessings of gospel living, we naturally want to share those blessings with others. The Lord spoke of the joy that comes into our lives when we share His gospel:

"If it so be that you should labor all your days in crying repentance unto this people, and bring, save it be one soul unto me, how great shall be your joy with him in the kingdom of my Father!

"And now, if your joy will be great with one soul that you have brought unto me into the kingdom of my Father, how great will be your joy if you should bring many souls unto me!" (D&C 18:15–16).

## Each Member's Missionary Duty

The Lord has declared that missionary work is the responsibility of all Latter-day Saints (see D&C 88:81). As a member of the Lord's Church, you can, by the goodness of your life and the strength of your testimony, help prepare your family members, friends, and other acquaintances to meet with the full-time missionaries.

The most powerful missionary message you can send is your own example of living a happy Latter-day Saint life. Remember that people do not join the Church only because of gospel principles they learn. They join because they feel something that begins to satisfy their spiritual needs. If you are sincere in your friendship with them, they will be able to feel the spirit of your testimony and happiness.

In addition to setting a good example, you can "be ready always to give an answer to every man that asketh you a reason of the hope that is in you" (1 Peter 3:15). You can pray for opportunities to tell others about the restored gospel. Then you can be alert, because many people yearn for the truth.

## Serving Full-Time Missions

After His Resurrection, the Lord commanded His disciples to "go . . . and teach all nations, baptizing them in the name of the Father, and of the Son, and of the Holy Ghost" (Matthew 28:19). In fulfillment of this command, able young men in the Church have a duty to prepare spiritually, physically, and emotionally to serve as full-time missionaries. Single women and mature couples also have the opportunity to serve full-time missions. If you desire to serve a full-time mission, speak with your bishop or branch president.

Ministering to New Members of the Church

Missionary work includes helping and supporting those who join the Church. As you ponder this responsibility, remember that new members may face trials when they join the Church. Their new commitments often require them to set aside old habits and leave old friends and associations. In addition, the Church introduces a way of life that may seem different and demanding.

Each new member of the Church needs three things: a friend, a responsibility, and nurturing with "the good word of God" (Moroni 6:4). You can be part of the effort to provide this help. You can always be a friend. Even if you are not in a position to extend formal Church callings or responsibilities, you can work beside new members in acts of service. And you can seek opportunities to share the word of God with new members.

Additional references: Mark 16:15; Alma 26:1–16; D&C 4; 60:2; 84:88; 123:12

# Modesty

Modesty is an attitude of humility and decency in dress, grooming, language, and behavior. If you are modest, you do not draw undue attention to yourself. Instead, you seek to "glorify God in your body, and in your spirit" (1 Corinthians 6:20; see also verse 19).

If you are unsure about whether your dress or grooming is modest, ask yourself, "Would I feel comfortable with my appearance if I were in the Lord's presence?" You might ask yourself a similar question about your language and behavior: "Would I say these words or participate in these activities if the Lord were present?" Your honest answers to these questions may lead you to make important changes in your life. The following information will help you in your efforts to be modest.

Dress and Grooming

Prophets have always counseled us to dress modestly. This counsel is founded on the truth that the human body is God's sacred creation. Respect your body as a gift from God. Through your dress and appearance, you can show the Lord that you know how precious your body is.

Your clothing expresses who you are. It sends messages about you, and it influences the way you and others act. When you are well groomed and modestly dressed, you can invite the companionship of the Spirit and exercise a good influence on those around you.

Central to the command to be modest is an understanding of the sacred power of procreation, the ability to bring children into the world. This power is to be used only between husband and wife. Revealing and sexually suggestive clothing, which includes short shorts and skirts, tight clothing, and shirts that do not cover the stomach, can stimulate desires and actions that violate the Lord's law of chastity.

In addition to avoiding clothing that is revealing, you should avoid extremes in clothing, appearance, and hairstyle. In dress, grooming, and manners, always be neat and clean, never sloppy or inappropriately casual. Do not disfigure yourself with tattoos or body piercings. If you are a woman and you desire to have your ears pierced, wear only one pair of modest earrings.

Maintain high standards of modesty for all occasions. Do not lower your standards to draw attention to your body or to seek approval from others. True disciples of Jesus Christ maintain the Lord's standard regardless of current fashions or pressure from others.

Language and Behavior

Like your dress and grooming, your language and behavior are expressions of your character. Your words and actions can have a profound influence on you and on others. Express yourself through clean, positive, uplifting language and in actions that bring happiness to those around you. Your efforts to be modest in word and deed lead to increased guidance and comfort from the Holy Ghost.

Avoid the filthy language and the casual, irreverent use of the Lord's name that are so common in the world. Withstand any temptation to participate in extreme or inappropriate behavior. The irreverent nature of such language and behavior impairs your ability to receive the quiet promptings of the Holy Ghost.

Additional references: D&C 42:40–41; Articles of Faith 1:13

*See also* Body Piercing; Chastity; Profanity; Tattooing

## Obedience

In the premortal existence, Heavenly Father presided over a great Council in Heaven. There we learned of His plan for our salvation, which included a time of testing on the earth: "We will make an earth whereon these may dwell; and we will prove them herewith, to see if they will do all things whatsoever the Lord their God shall command them" (Abraham 3:24–25). One reason you are here on the earth is to show your willingness to obey Heavenly Father's commandments.

Many people feel that the commandments are burdensome and that they limit freedom and personal growth. But the Savior taught that true freedom comes only from following Him: "If ye continue in my word, then are ye my disciples indeed; and ye shall know the truth, and the truth shall make you free" (John 8:31–32). God gives commandments for your benefit. They are loving instructions for your happiness and your physical and spiritual well-being.

The Prophet Joseph Smith taught that obedience to the commandments leads to blessings from God. He said: "There is a law, irrevocably decreed in heaven before the foundations of this world, upon which all blessings are predicated—and when we obtain any blessing from God, it is by obedience to that law upon which it is predicated" (D&C 130:20–21). King Benjamin also taught this principle. "I would desire that ye should consider on the blessed and happy state of those that keep the commandments of God," he counseled. "For behold, they are blessed in all things, both temporal and spiritual; and if they hold out faithful to the end they are received into heaven, that thereby they may dwell with God in a state of never-ending happiness. O remember, remember that these things are true; for the Lord God hath spoken it" (Mosiah 2:41).

Our obedience to the commandments is an expression of our love for Heavenly Father and Jesus Christ. The Savior said, "If ye love me, keep my commandments" (John 14:15). He later declared: "If ye keep my commandments, ye shall abide in my love; even as I have kept my Father's commandments, and abide in his love" (John 15:10).

Additional references: Joshua 24:14–15; Ecclesiastes 12:13; Matthew 7:21; John 7:17; 1 Nephi 3:7; D&C 58:21–22; 82:8–10

*See also* Agency; Plan of Salvation

## Ordinances

In the Church, an ordinance is a sacred, formal act performed by the authority of the priesthood. Some ordinances are essential to our exaltation. These ordinances are called saving ordinances. They include baptism, confirmation, ordination to the Melchizedek Priesthood (for men), the temple endowment, and the marriage sealing. With each of these ordinances, we enter into solemn covenants with the Lord.

Other ordinances, such as naming and blessing children, consecrating oil, and administering to the sick and afflicted, are also performed by priesthood authority. While they are not essential to our salvation, they are important for our comfort, guidance, and encouragement.

Ordinances and covenants help us remember who we are. They remind us of our duty to God. The Lord has provided them to help us come unto Him and receive eternal life. When we honor them, He strengthens us.

You may receive many opportunities to participate in priesthood ordinances. Whenever you have such an opportunity, do all you can to prepare yourself, whether you are performing the ordinance or receiving it. You can prepare by praying, fasting, counseling with priesthood leaders, and studying the scriptures and the words of latter-day prophets. If you are a priesthood holder, you should always be spiritually prepared to perform an ordinance. Live a clean, worthy life, and strive to receive the constant companionship of the Holy Ghost.

Additional references: D&C 84:19–21; Articles of Faith 1:3–5

*See also* Covenant; Gospel; Priesthood

## Original Sin

Because of the Fall of Adam and Eve, all people live in a fallen condition, separated from God and subject to physical death. However, we are not condemned by what many call the "original sin." In other words, we are not accountable for Adam's transgression in the Garden of Eden. The Prophet Joseph Smith said, "We believe that men will be punished for their own sins, and not for Adam's transgression" (Articles of Faith 1:2).

Through the Atonement, the Savior paid the price for the transgression in the Garden of Eden (see Moses 6:53). He has given us the assurance of resurrection and the promise that, based on our faithfulness, we can return to dwell in the presence of our Heavenly Father forever.

*See also* Fall

## Paradise

In the scriptures, the word *paradise* is used in different ways. First, it designates a place of peace and happiness in the postmortal spirit world, reserved for those who have been baptized and who have remained faithful (see Alma 40:12; Moroni 10:34). Those in spirit prison have the opportunity to learn the gospel of Jesus Christ, repent of their sins, and receive the ordinances of baptism and confirmation through the work we do in temples (see D&C 138:30–35). When they do, they may enter paradise.

A second use of the word *paradise* is found in Luke's account of the Savior's Crucifixion. When Jesus was on the cross, a thief who also was being crucified said, "Lord, remember me when thou comest into thy kingdom" (Luke 23:42). According to Luke 23:43, the Lord replied, "Verily I say unto thee, To day shalt thou be with me in paradise." The Prophet Joseph Smith explained that this is a mistranslation; the Lord actually said that the thief would be with Him in the world of spirits.

The word *paradise* is also found in 2 Corinthians 12:4, where it probably refers to the celestial kingdom. In the tenth article of faith, the word *paradisiacal* describes the earth's glory in the Millennium.

*See also* Death, Physical; Plan of Salvation; Resurrection

## Patriarchal Blessings

Patriarchal blessings are given to worthy members of the Church by ordained patriarchs. Your patriarchal blessing declares your lineage in the house of Israel and contains personal counsel from the Lord to you.

As you study your patriarchal blessing and follow the counsel it contains, it will provide guidance, comfort, and protection. To find out how to receive a patriarchal blessing, talk with your bishop or branch president.

## Declaration of Lineage

Your patriarchal blessing includes a declaration of your lineage, stating that you are of the house of Israel—a descendant of Abraham, belonging to a specific tribe of Jacob. Many Latter-day Saints are of the tribe of Ephraim, the tribe given the primary responsibility to lead the latter-day work of the Lord.

Because each of us has many bloodlines running in us, two members of the same family may be declared as being of different tribes in Israel.

It does not matter if your lineage in the house of Israel is through bloodlines or by adoption. As a member of the Church, you are counted as a descendant of Abraham and an heir to all the promises and blessings contained in the Abrahamic covenant (see "Abrahamic Covenant," pages 5–6).

## Learning from Your Patriarchal Blessing

Once you have received your patriarchal blessing, you should read it humbly, prayerfully, and frequently. It is a personal revelation from your Heavenly Father, who knows your strengths, weaknesses, and eternal potential. Through your patriarchal blessing, He will help you learn what He expects of you. Your blessing may contain promises, admonitions, and warnings. As time goes on, you will recognize the power of the revelation in it.

As you follow the counsel in your blessing, you will be less likely to stumble or be misled. If you do not follow the counsel, you will not be able to receive the promised blessings.

While your patriarchal blessing contains inspired counsel and promises, you should not expect it to answer all your questions or to detail all that will happen in your life. If your blessing does not mention an important event, such as a full-time mission or marriage, you should not assume that you will not receive that opportunity.

Similarly, you should not assume that everything mentioned in your patriarchal blessing will be fulfilled in this life. A patriarchal blessing is eternal, and its promises may extend into the eternities. Be assured that if you are worthy, all promises will be fulfilled in the Lord's due time. Those that are not realized in this life will be fulfilled in the next.

Your patriarchal blessing is sacred and personal. You may share it with immediate family members, but you should not read it aloud in public or permit others to read it or interpret it. Not even your patriarch or bishop or branch president should interpret it.

Treasure in your heart the precious words in your patriarchal blessing. Ponder them, and live so that you will be worthy to receive the promised blessings in this life and in the life to come.

## Peace

Many people think of peace as the absence of war. But we can feel peace even in times of war, and we can lack peace even when no war is raging. The mere absence of conflict is not enough to bring peace to our hearts. Peace comes through the gospel—through the Atonement of Jesus Christ, the ministration of the Holy Ghost, and our own righteousness, sincere repentance, and diligent service.

Even when the world is in turmoil all around you, you can receive the blessing of inner peace. This blessing will continue with you as you stay true to your testimony of the gospel and as you remember that Heavenly Father and Jesus Christ love you and watch over you.

In addition to feeling peace yourself, you can be an influence for peace in your family, your community, and the world.

You work for peace when you keep the commandments, give service, care for family members and neighbors, and share the gospel. You work for peace whenever you help relieve the suffering of another.

The following words of the Savior teach us how we can experience the peace that the gospel brings:

"The Comforter, which is the Holy Ghost, whom the Father will send in my name, he shall teach you all things, and bring all things to your remembrance, whatsoever I have said unto you.

"Peace I leave with you, my peace I give unto you: not as the world giveth, give I unto you. Let not your heart be troubled, neither let it be afraid" (John 14:26–27).

"Fear not to do good, my sons, for whatsoever ye sow, that shall ye also reap; therefore, if ye sow good ye shall also reap good for your reward.

"Therefore, fear not, little flock; do good; let earth and hell combine against you, for if ye are built upon my rock, they cannot prevail.

"Behold, I do not condemn you; go your ways and sin no more; perform with soberness the work which I have commanded you.

"Look unto me in every thought; doubt not, fear not.

"Behold the wounds which pierced my side, and also the prints of the nails in my hands and feet; be faithful, keep my commandments, and ye shall inherit the kingdom of heaven" (D&C 6:33–37).

"These things I have spoken unto you, that in me ye might have peace. In the world ye shall have tribulation: but be of good cheer; I have overcome the world" (John 16:33).

As you remember the Savior and follow Him, you truly can be of good cheer. You can experience real, enduring peace at all times. You can find hope in the Savior's first words to His disciples after His Resurrection: "Peace be unto you" (John 20:19).

Additional reference: D&C 59:23

*See also* Charity; Holy Ghost; Hope; Jesus Christ; Love; Service; War

## Pearl of Great Price *(See* Scriptures)

## Personal Revelation *(See* Revelation)

## Plan of Salvation

In the premortal existence, Heavenly Father prepared a plan to enable us to become like Him and receive a fulness of joy. The scriptures refer to this plan as "the plan of salvation" (Alma 24:14; Moses 6:62), "the great plan of happiness" (Alma 42:8), "the plan of redemption" (Jacob 6:8; Alma 12:30), and "the plan of mercy" (Alma 42:15).

The plan of salvation is the fulness of the gospel. It includes the Creation, the Fall, the Atonement of Jesus Christ, and all the laws, ordinances, and doctrines of the gospel. Moral agency, the ability to choose and act for ourselves, is also essential in Heavenly Father's plan. Because of this plan, we can be perfected through the Atonement, receive a fulness of joy, and live forever in the presence of God. Our family relationships can last throughout the eternities.

You are a participant in Heavenly Father's plan, and your eternal experience can be divided into three main parts: premortal life, mortal life, and life after death. As you come to understand the plan, you find answers to questions asked by so many: Where did we come from? Why are we here? Where do we go after this life?

### Premortal Life

Before you were born on the earth, you lived in the presence of your Heavenly Father as one of His spirit children. In this premortal existence, you attended a council with Heavenly Father's other spirit children. At that council,

Heavenly Father presented His great plan of happiness (see Abraham 3:22–26).

In harmony with the plan of happiness, the premortal Jesus Christ, the Firstborn Son of the Father in the spirit, covenanted to be the Savior (see Moses 4:2; Abraham 3:27). Those who followed Heavenly Father and Jesus Christ were permitted to come to the earth to experience mortality and progress toward eternal life. Lucifer, another spirit son of God, rebelled against the plan and "sought to destroy the agency of man" (Moses 4:3). He became Satan, and he and his followers were cast out of heaven and denied the privileges of receiving a physical body and experiencing mortality (see Moses 4:4; Abraham 3:27–28).

Throughout your premortal life, you developed your identity and increased your spiritual capabilities. Blessed with the gift of agency, you made important decisions, such as the decision to follow Heavenly Father's plan. These decisions affected your life then and now. You grew in intelligence and learned to love the truth, and you prepared to come to the earth, where you could continue to progress.

Mortal Life

You are now experiencing mortal life. Your spirit is united with your body, giving you opportunities to grow and develop in ways that were not possible in your premortal life. This part of your existence is a time of learning in which you can prove yourself, choose to come unto Christ, and prepare to be worthy of eternal life. It is also a time when you can help others find the truth and gain a testimony of the plan of salvation.

Life after Death

When you die, your spirit will enter the spirit world and await the resurrection. At the time of the resurrection, your spirit and body will reunite, and you will be judged and received into a kingdom of glory. The glory you inherit will depend on the depth of your conversion and your obedience to the Lord's commandments (see "Kingdoms of Glory," pages 92–95). It will depend on the manner in which you have "received the testimony of Jesus" (D&C 76:51; see also verses 74, 79, 101).

Blessings through Knowledge of the Plan

A testimony of the plan of salvation can give you hope and purpose as you wrestle with the challenges of life. You can find reassurance in the knowledge that you are a child of God and that you lived in His presence before you were born on the earth. You can find meaning in your present life, knowing that your actions during mortality influence your eternal destiny. With this knowledge, you can base important decisions on eternal truths rather than on the changing circumstances of life. You can continually improve your relationship with family members, rejoicing in the promise that your family can be eternal. You can find joy in your testimony of the Atonement and the Lord's commandments, ordinances, covenants, and doctrines, knowing that "he who doeth the works of righteousness shall receive his reward, even peace in this world, and eternal life in the world to come" (D&C 59:23).

Additional references: 2 Nephi 2:5–30; 10:23–25; Alma 12:24–37; 22:12–14; 42; Moses 6:47–62

*See also* Agency; Atonement of Jesus Christ; Creation; Death, Physical; Death, Spiritual; Fall; God the Father; Gospel; Heaven; Hell; Jesus Christ; Kingdoms of Glory; Paradise; Resurrection

# Pornography

Pornography is any material depicting or describing the human body or sexual conduct in a way that arouses sexual feelings. It is distributed through many media, including magazines, books, television, movies, music, and the Internet. It is as harmful to the spirit as tobacco, alcohol, and drugs are to the body. Using pornographic material in any way is a violation of a commandment of God: "Thou shalt not . . . commit adultery . . . nor do anything like unto it" (D&C 59:6). It can lead to other serious sins. Members of the Church should avoid pornography in any form and should oppose its production, distribution, and use.

Pornography is tragically addictive. Like other addictions, it leads people to experiment and to seek more powerful stimulations. If you experiment with it and allow yourself to remain caught in its trap, it will destroy you, degrading your mind, heart, and spirit. It will rob you of self-respect and of your sense of the beauties of life. It will tear you down and lead you to evil thoughts and possibly evil actions. It will cause terrible damage to your family relationships.

Because of the addictive nature of pornography and the harm it can cause to body and spirit, servants of God have repeatedly warned us to shun it. If you are caught in the trap of pornography, stop immediately and seek help. Through repentance, you can receive forgiveness and find hope in the gospel. Go to your bishop or branch president for counsel on how to overcome your problem, and seek healing through the Atonement of Jesus Christ. Ask the Lord to give you the strength to overcome this terrible addiction.

Additional references: Matthew 5:27–28; Romans 6:12; Alma 39:9; D&C 42:23

*See also* Chastity; Temptation

## Prayer

You are a child of God. Your Heavenly Father loves you and knows your needs, and He wants you to communicate with Him through prayer. Pray to Him and no one else. The Lord Jesus Christ commanded, "Ye must always pray unto the Father in my name" (3 Nephi 18:19).

As you make a habit of approaching God in prayer, you will come to know Him and draw ever nearer to Him. Your desires will become more like His. You will be able to secure for yourself and for others blessings that He is ready to give if you will but ask in faith.

Principles of Prayer

Your Heavenly Father is always ready to hear and answer your prayers. The power of your prayers depends on you. As you strive to make prayer a part of your life, remember this counsel:

*Make your prayers meaningful.* The prophet Mormon warned that if anyone "shall pray and not with real intent of heart . . . it profiteth him nothing, for God receiveth none such" (Moroni 7:9). To make your prayers meaningful, you must pray with sincerity and "with all the energy of heart" (Moroni 7:48). Be careful to avoid "vain repetitions" when you pray (see Matthew 6:7). Give serious thought to your attitude and to the words you use.

*Use language that shows love, respect, reverence, and closeness.* The application of this principle will vary according to the language you speak. If you pray in English, for example, you should use the pronouns of the scriptures when you address God—*Thee, Thou, Thy,* and *Thine,* rather than the more common pronouns *you, your,* and *yours.* Regardless of the language, the principle remains the same: When you pray, you should use words that appropriately convey a loving, worshipful relationship with God. You may have some difficulty learning the language of prayer, but you will gradually become more comfortable with it as you pray and read the scriptures.

*Always give thanks to your Heavenly Father.* You should "live in thanksgiving daily, for the many mercies and blessings which he doth bestow upon you" (Alma 34:38). As you take time to remember your blessings, you will recognize how much your Heavenly Father has done for you. Express your thanks to Him.

*Seek Heavenly Father's guidance and strength in all you do.* Alma counseled his son Helaman: "Cry unto God for all thy support; yea, let all thy doings be unto the Lord, and whithersoever thou goest let it be in the Lord; yea, let all thy thoughts be directed unto the Lord; yea, let the affections of thy heart be placed upon the Lord forever. Counsel with the Lord in all thy doings, and he will direct thee for good; yea, when thou liest down at night lie down unto the Lord, that he may watch over you in your sleep; and when thou risest in the morning let thy heart be full of thanks unto God; and if ye do these things, ye shall be lifted up at the last day" (Alma 37:36–37; see also Alma 34:17–26).

*Remember the needs of others as you pray.* Offer prayers "for your welfare, and also for the welfare of those who are around you" (Alma 34:27). Ask your Heavenly Father to bless and comfort those in need. Ask Him to inspire and strengthen the President of the Church, other General Authorities, and your local Church leaders. Pray for the welfare of family members and friends. Pray for government leaders. Ask the Lord to inspire and protect the missionaries and the people they are teaching.

*Seek the guidance of the Holy Ghost so you will know what to include in your prayers.* The Holy Ghost can teach you to pray and guide you in the things you say (see Romans 8:26; 2 Nephi 32:8). He can help you pray "according to the will of God" (D&C 46:30).

*When you make a request through prayer, do all you can to assist in its being granted.* Heavenly Father expects you to do more than merely ask Him for blessings. When you have an important decision to make, He often will require that you "study it out in your mind" before He will give you an answer (see D&C 9:7–8). Your prayers for guidance will be only as effective as your efforts to be receptive to the whisperings of the Holy Ghost. Your prayers for your own welfare and for the welfare of others will be in vain if you "turn away the needy, and the naked, and visit not the sick and afflicted, and impart of your substance, if ye have, to those who stand in need" (Alma 34:28).

If you have a difficult task before you, Heavenly Father is pleased when you get on your knees and ask for help and then get on your feet and go to work. He will help you in all your righteous pursuits, but He seldom will do something for you that you can do yourself.

Personal Prayer

In His Sermon on the Mount, Jesus Christ counseled: "Enter into thy closet, and when thou hast shut thy door, pray to thy Father which is in secret; and thy Father which seeth in secret shall reward thee openly" (Matthew 6:6). Personal, private prayer is an essential part of your spiritual development.

At least every morning and every night, find a place that is free from distractions. Kneel in humility and commune with your Heavenly Father. Although sometimes you may need to pray silently, make an extra effort at times to pray vocally (see D&C 19:28; 20:51).

Remember that prayer is two-way communication. As you close your prayers, take time to pause and listen. At times, Heavenly Father will counsel, guide, or comfort you while you are on your knees.

Never give in to the idea that you are not worthy to pray. This idea comes from Satan, who wants to convince you that you must not pray (see 2 Nephi 32:8). If you do not feel like praying, pray until you do feel like praying.

The Savior has commanded, "Pray always, that you may come off conqueror; yea, that you may conquer Satan, and that you may escape the hands of the servants of Satan that do uphold his work" (D&C 10:5). Although you cannot be continuously on your knees, always offering a personal, private prayer, you can let your heart be "full, drawn out in prayer unto [God] continually" (Alma 34:27; see also 3 Nephi 20:1). Throughout each day, you can maintain a constant feeling of love for your Heavenly Father and His Beloved Son. You can silently express gratitude to your Father and ask Him to strengthen you in your responsibilities. In times of temptation or physical danger, you can silently ask for His help.

## Family Prayer

In addition to commanding us to pray in private, the Savior has exhorted us to pray with our families. He said, "Pray in your families unto the Father, always in my name, that your wives and your children may be blessed" (3 Nephi 18:21).

If you are married, make family prayer a consistent part of your family's life. Every morning and every evening, kneel together in humility. Give each family member frequent opportunities to say the prayer. Unite in gratitude for the blessings Heavenly Father has given you. Unite in faith to plead for the blessings you need and to pray for others.

Through regular family prayer, you and your family members will draw nearer to God and to each other. Your children will learn to communicate with their Father in Heaven. You will all be better prepared to serve others and withstand temptations. Your home will be a place of spiritual strength, a refuge from the evil influences of the world.

## Public Prayer

At times you may be asked to offer a public prayer, perhaps in a Church meeting or class. When you receive this opportunity, remember that you are communicating with

Heavenly Father, not giving a public sermon. Do not worry about what others may think of what you say. Instead, offer a simple, heartfelt prayer.

Receiving Answers to Prayer

The Savior taught, "Ask, and it shall be given you; seek, and ye shall find; knock, and it shall be opened unto you: for every one that asketh receiveth; and he that seeketh findeth; and to him that knocketh it shall be opened" (Matthew 7:7–8). To the Nephites He said, "Whatsoever ye shall ask the Father in my name, which is right, believing that ye shall receive, behold it shall be given unto you" (3 Nephi 18:20).

Heavenly Father hears your prayers. He may not always answer as you expect, but He does answer—in His own time and according to His will. Because He knows what is best for you, He may sometimes answer *no*, even when your petitions are sincere.

Answers to prayer come in many ways. They often come through the still, small voice of the Holy Ghost (see "Revelation," pages 140–44). They may come in the circumstances of your life or through the kind acts of those around you. As you continue to draw near to your Heavenly Father through prayer, you will recognize more readily His merciful and wise answers to your pleadings. You will find that He is your "refuge and strength, a very present help in trouble" (Psalm 46:1).

Additional references: Matthew 6:5–15; James 1:5–6; Enos 1:1–17; Mosiah 4:11–12; 3 Nephi 13:6–7; 14:7–8; D&C 19:38; 88:63–65; Joseph Smith— History 1:9–19

*See also* Faith; Fasting and Fast Offerings; Worship

**Premortal Existence** (*See* Plan of Salvation)

**Priest** (*See* Aaronic Priesthood; Church Administration; Priesthood)

# Priesthood

The priesthood is the eternal power and authority of God. Through the priesthood God created and governs the heavens and the earth. Through this power He redeems and exalts His children, bringing to pass "the immortality and eternal life of man" (Moses 1:39).

## Priesthood Authority Given to Men on Earth

God gives priesthood authority to worthy male members of the Church so they can act in His name for the salvation of His children. Priesthood holders can be authorized to preach the gospel, administer the ordinances of salvation, and govern the kingdom of God on the earth.

Male members of the Church may begin their priesthood service when they reach the age of 12. They begin by holding the Aaronic Priesthood, and they later may qualify to have the Melchizedek Priesthood conferred on them. At different stages in their lives and as they prepare themselves to receive different responsibilities, they hold different offices in the priesthood, such as deacon, teacher, or priest in the Aaronic Priesthood and elder or high priest in the Melchizedek Priesthood. (For specific information about the Aaronic and Melchizedek Priesthoods, see pages 3–4 and 101–2.)

For a male member of the Church to hold the priesthood, an authorized priesthood holder must confer it on him and ordain him to an office in that priesthood (see Hebrews 5:4; D&C 42:11; Articles of Faith 1:5).

Although the authority of the priesthood is bestowed only on worthy male members of the Church, the blessings of the priesthood are available to all—men, women, and children. We all benefit from the influence of righteous priesthood leadership, and we all have the privilege of receiving the saving ordinances of the priesthood.

Priesthood and the Family

The most important exercise of the priesthood takes place in the family. Each husband and father in the Church should strive to be worthy to hold the Melchizedek Priesthood. With his wife as an equal partner, he presides in righteousness and love, serving as the family's spiritual leader. He leads the family in regular prayer, scripture study, and family home evening. He works with his wife to teach the children and help them prepare to receive the ordinances of salvation (see D&C 68:25–28). He gives priesthood blessings for direction, healing, and comfort.

Many members do not have faithful Melchizedek Priesthood holders in their homes. However, through the service of home teachers and priesthood leaders, all members of the Church can enjoy the blessings of priesthood power in their lives.

Priesthood Quorums

A priesthood quorum is an organized group of brethren who hold the same priesthood office. The primary purposes of quorums are to serve others, build unity and brotherhood, and instruct one another in doctrines, principles, and duties.

Quorums exist at all levels of Church organization. The President of the Church and his counselors form the Quorum of the First Presidency. The Twelve Apostles also form a quorum. Seventies, both General Authorities and Area Authorities, are organized into quorums. Each stake president presides over a quorum of high priests, made up of all the high priests in the stake. Each ward or branch normally has quorums of elders, priests, teachers, and deacons. High priests are also organized in wards, serving in high priests groups.

Home Teaching

From the time priesthood holders are ordained to the office of teacher, they have the opportunity and responsibility to serve as home teachers. In this way they work toward ful-filling their duty to "watch over the church always, and be with and strengthen them" (D&C 20:53).

Home teachers have a sacred duty to be the Church's first source of help to individuals and families. They visit their assigned members at least monthly. In serving and visiting their assigned members, they support parents in their respon-sibilities, teach the gospel to each family member, nurture friendships, and help members prepare to receive temple ordinances and live worthy of the blessings of the gospel.

Leaders in wards and branches ensure that home teach-ers are assigned to each family or individual. They follow up with home teachers to help meet each member's spiritual and temporal needs.

## Priesthood Keys

The exercise of priesthood authority in the Church is gov-erned by those who hold priesthood keys (see D&C 65:2; 124:123). Those who hold priesthood keys have the right to preside over and direct the Church within a jurisdiction. For example, a bishop holds priesthood keys that enable him to preside in his ward. Therefore, when a child in that ward is prepared to be baptized, the person baptizing the child must receive authorization from the bishop.

Jesus Christ holds all the keys of the priesthood. He has given His Apostles the keys that are necessary for governing His Church. Only the senior Apostle, the President of the Church, may use (or authorize another person to use) these keys for governing the entire Church (see D&C 43:1–4; 81:2; 132:7).

The President of the Church delegates priesthood keys to other priesthood leaders so they can preside in their areas of responsibility. Priesthood keys are bestowed on presidents of temples, missions, stakes, and districts; bishops; branch presidents; and quorum presidents. A person who serves in one of these positions holds the keys only until he is released.

Counselors do not receive keys, but they do receive authority and responsibility by calling and assignment.

## Exercising the Priesthood Righteously

If you are a priesthood holder, remember that the priesthood should be a part of you at all times and in all circumstances. It is not like a cloak that you can put on and take off at will. Any ordination to a priesthood office is a call to lifelong service, with the promise that the Lord will qualify you to do His work according to your faithfulness.

You must be worthy in order to receive and exercise priesthood power. The words you speak and your everyday behavior affect your ability to serve. Your behavior in public must be above reproach. Your behavior in private is even more important. Through the Prophet Joseph Smith, the Lord declared that "the rights of the priesthood are inseparably connected with the powers of heaven, and that the powers of heaven cannot be controlled nor handled only upon the principles of righteousness" (D&C 121:36). He warned priesthood holders:

"When we undertake to cover our sins, or to gratify our pride, our vain ambition, or to exercise control or dominion or compulsion upon the souls of the children of men, in any degree of unrighteousness, behold, the heavens withdraw themselves; the Spirit of the Lord is grieved; and when it is withdrawn, Amen to the priesthood or the authority of that man. Behold, ere he is aware, he is left unto himself" (D&C 121:37–38).

You cannot maintain any power or influence in the priesthood except "by persuasion, by long-suffering, by gentleness and meekness, and by love unfeigned; by kindness, and pure knowledge, which shall greatly enlarge the soul without hypocrisy, and without guile." If you are "moved upon by the Holy Ghost" to reprove someone, show forth afterward "an increase of love toward him whom thou hast reproved, lest he esteem thee to be his enemy; that he may know that thy faithfulness is stronger than the cords of death" (D&C 121:41–43).

As you exercise the priesthood in righteousness and love, you will find joy in serving as an instrument in the Lord's hands. He said:

"Let thy bowels also be full of charity towards all men, and to the household of faith, and let virtue garnish thy thoughts unceasingly; then shall thy confidence wax strong in the presence of God; and the doctrine of the priesthood shall distil upon thy soul as the dews from heaven.

"The Holy Ghost shall be thy constant companion, and thy scepter an unchanging scepter of righteousness and truth; and thy dominion shall be an everlasting dominion, and without compulsory means it shall flow unto thee forever and ever" (D&C 121:45–46).

Additional references: John 15:16; Acts 8:14–20; James 5:14–15; D&C 13; 20; 84; 107; Joseph Smith—History 1:68–73

*See also* Aaronic Priesthood; Church Administration; Melchizedek Priesthood; Ordinances; Restoration of the Gospel

## Profanity

Profanity is disrespect or contempt for sacred things. It includes casual or irreverent use of the name of any member of the Godhead. It also includes any type of unclean or vulgar speech or behavior.

Always use the names of Heavenly Father, Jesus Christ, and the Holy Ghost with reverence and respect. Misusing their names is a sin. Profane, vulgar, or crude language or gestures, as well as immoral jokes, are offensive to the Lord and to others.

Foul language harms your spirit and degrades you. Do not let others influence you to use foul language. Instead, use clean language that uplifts and edifies others. Choose friends who use good language. Set an example that will encourage those around you to use clean language. If friends and acquaintances use profanity, good-naturedly encourage them to choose other words. If they persist, politely walk away or change the subject.

If you have developed the habit of swearing, you can break it. Begin by making a decision to change. Pray for help. If you are tempted to use profane language, keep quiet or say what you have to say in a different way.

Additional references: Leviticus 19:12; D&C 63:60–64

*See also* Modesty; Temptation

**Prophecy** (*See* Revelation; Spiritual Gifts)

## Prophets

As members of The Church of Jesus Christ of Latter-day Saints, we are blessed to be led by living prophets—inspired men called to speak for the Lord, just as Moses, Isaiah, Peter, Paul, Nephi, Mormon, and other prophets of the scriptures. We sustain the President of the Church as our prophet, seer, and revelator—the only person on the earth who receives revelation to guide the entire Church. We also sustain the counselors in the First Presidency and the members of the Quorum of the Twelve Apostles as prophets, seers, and revelators.

Like the prophets of old, prophets today testify of Jesus Christ and teach His gospel. They make known God's will and true character. They speak boldly and clearly, denouncing sin and warning of its consequences. At times, they may be inspired to prophesy of future events for our benefit.

You can always trust the living prophets. Their teachings reflect the will of the Lord, who declared: "What I the Lord have spoken, I have spoken, and I excuse not myself; and though the heavens and the earth pass away, my word shall not pass away, but shall all be fulfilled, whether by mine own voice or by the voice of my servants, it is the same" (D&C 1:38).

Your greatest safety lies in strictly following the word of the Lord given through His prophets, particularly the current President of the Church. The Lord warns that those who ignore the words of the living prophets will fall (see D&C 1:14–16). He promises great blessings to those who follow the President of the Church:

"Thou shalt give heed unto all his words and commandments which he shall give unto you as he receiveth them, walking in all holiness before me;

"For his word ye shall receive, as if from mine own mouth, in all patience and faith.

"For by doing these things the gates of hell shall not prevail against you; yea, and the Lord God will disperse the powers of darkness from before you, and cause the heavens to shake for your good, and his name's glory" (D&C 21:4–6).

Additional references: 2 Chronicles 20:20; Amos 3:7; Ephesians 2:19–20; 1 Nephi 22:1–2; Mosiah 13:33–35; D&C 107:91–92; Articles of Faith 1:6

## Quorum *(See* Priesthood)

## Quorum of the Twelve Apostles *(See* Church Administration)

## Quorums of the Seventy *(See* Church Administration)

## Relief Society

The Relief Society was founded by the Prophet Joseph Smith on March 17, 1842, in Nauvoo, Illinois. In the days of its founding, the Relief Society had two main purposes: to provide relief for the poor and needy and to save souls. The organization continues today, staying true to those original guiding principles. Throughout the world, sisters in the Relief Society work with priesthood holders to carry out the mission of the Church. They support one another as they:

- Increase their testimonies of Jesus Christ through prayer and scripture study.
- Seek spiritual strength by following the promptings of the Holy Ghost.
- Dedicate themselves to strengthening marriages, families, and homes.
- Find nobility in motherhood and joy in womanhood.
- Delight in service and good works.
- Love life and learning.
- Stand for truth and righteousness.
- Sustain the priesthood as the authority of God on the earth.
- Rejoice in the blessings of the temple.
- Understand their divine destiny and strive for exaltation.

If you are in the Relief Society, one way you can contribute to the mission of the organization is to accept an assignment to serve as a visiting teacher. As you visit and serve your assigned sisters, take time to teach the gospel and nurture friendships. In addition to serving individuals, you can play an important role in strengthening families.

Leaders in wards and branches ensure that visiting teachers are assigned to each sister age 18 or older. Priesthood and Relief Society leaders follow up with visiting teachers to help meet each sister's spiritual and temporal needs.

As a sister in Relief Society, you are a member of a worldwide sisterhood, united in devotion to Jesus Christ. You join with other daughters of God as a woman of faith, virtue, vision, and charity, with the sure knowledge that your life has meaning, purpose, and direction. Through your participation in Relief Society, you have opportunities to enjoy sisterhood and companionship, give meaningful service, share your testimony and your talents, and grow spiritually.

# Repentance

Repentance is one of the first principles of the gospel (see Articles of Faith 1:4). It is essential to your happiness in this life and throughout eternity. Repentance is much more than just acknowledging wrongdoings. It is a change of mind and heart that gives you a fresh view about God, about yourself, and about the world. It includes turning away from sin and turning to God for forgiveness. It is motivated by love for God and the sincere desire to obey His commandments.

## The Need for Repentance

The Lord has declared that "no unclean thing can inherit the kingdom of heaven" (Alma 11:37). Your sins make you unclean—unworthy to return and dwell in the presence of your Heavenly Father. They also bring anguish to your soul in this life.

Through the Atonement of Jesus Christ, Heavenly Father has provided the only way for you to be forgiven of your sins (see "Forgiveness," pages 70–72). Jesus Christ suffered the penalty for your sins so you can be forgiven if you sincerely repent. As you repent and rely on His saving grace, you will be cleansed from sin. He declared:

"I command you to repent—repent, lest I smite you by the rod of my mouth, and by my wrath, and by my anger, and your sufferings be sore—how sore you know not, how exquisite you know not, yea, how hard to bear you know not.

"For behold, I, God, have suffered these things for all, that they might not suffer if they would repent;

"But if they would not repent they must suffer even as I;

"Which suffering caused myself, even God, the greatest of all, to tremble because of pain, and to bleed at every pore, and to suffer both body and spirit—and would that I might not drink the bitter cup, and shrink—

"Nevertheless, glory be to the Father, and I partook and finished my preparations unto the children of men" (D&C 19:15–19).

The Danger of Procrastinating Repentance

Do not rationalize your sins or put off repentance. Amulek warned: "This life is the time for men to prepare to meet God; yea, behold the day of this life is the day for men to perform their labors. . . . I beseech of you that ye do not procrastinate the day of your repentance until the end; for after this day of life, which is given us to prepare for eternity, behold, if we do not improve our time while in this life, then cometh the night of darkness wherein there can be no labor performed" (Alma 34:32–33).

Elements of Repentance

Repentance is a painful process, but it leads to forgiveness and lasting peace. Through the prophet Isaiah, the Lord said, "Though your sins be as scarlet, they shall be as white as snow; though they be red like crimson, they shall be as wool" (Isaiah 1:18). In this dispensation the Lord has promised, "He who has repented of his sins, the same is forgiven, and I, the Lord, remember them no more" (D&C 58:42). Repentance includes the following elements:

*Faith in Heavenly Father and Jesus Christ.* The power of sin is great. To become free from it, you must turn to your Heavenly Father and pray in faith. Satan may try to convince you that you are not worthy to pray—that Heavenly Father is so displeased with you that He will never hear your prayers. This is a lie. Your Father in Heaven is always ready to help you if you will come to Him with a repentant heart. He has the power to heal you and to help you triumph over sin.

Repentance is an act of faith in Jesus Christ—an acknowledgment of the power of His Atonement. Remember that you can be forgiven only on His terms. As you gratefully recognize His Atonement and His power to cleanse you from sin, you are able to "exercise your faith unto repentance" (Alma 34:17).

*Sorrow for Sin.* In order to be forgiven, you must first acknowledge within yourself that you have sinned. If you are striving to live the gospel, such an acknowledgment will lead to "godly sorrow," which "worketh repentance to salvation" (2 Corinthians 7:10). Godly sorrow does not come because of the natural consequences of sin or because of a fear of punishment; rather, it comes from the knowledge that you have displeased your Heavenly Father and your Savior. When you experience godly sorrow, you have a sincere desire for change and a willingness to submit to every requirement for forgiveness.

*Confession.* "He that covereth his sins shall not prosper: but whoso confesseth and forsaketh them shall have mercy" (Proverbs 28:13). Essential to forgiveness is a willingness to disclose fully to your Heavenly Father all that you have done. Kneel before Him in humble prayer, acknowledging your sins. Confess your shame and guilt, and then plead for help.

Serious transgressions, such as violations of the law of chastity, may jeopardize your membership in the Church. Therefore, you need to confess these sins to both the Lord and His representatives in the Church. This is done under the care of your bishop or branch president and possibly your stake or mission president, who serve as watchmen and judges in the Church. While only the Lord can forgive sins, these priesthood leaders play a critical role in the process of repentance. They will keep your confession confidential and help you throughout the process of repentance. Be completely honest with them. If you partially confess, mentioning only lesser mistakes, you will not be able to resolve a more serious, undisclosed transgression. The sooner you begin this process, the sooner you will find the peace and joy that come with the miracle of forgiveness.

*Abandonment of Sin.* Although confession is an essential element of repentance, it is not enough. The Lord has said, "By this ye may know if a man repenteth of his sins—behold, he will confess them and forsake them" (D&C 58:43).

Maintain an unyielding, permanent resolve that you will never repeat the transgression. When you keep this commitment, you will never experience the pain of that sin again.

Flee immediately from any dangerous situation. If a certain situation causes you to sin or may cause you to sin, leave. You cannot linger in temptation and expect to overcome sin.

*Restitution.* You must restore as far as possible all that has been damaged by your actions, whether that is someone's property or someone's good reputation. Willing restitution shows the Lord that you will do all you can to repent.

*Righteous Living.* It is not enough to simply try to resist evil or empty your life of sin. You must fill your life with righteousness and engage in activities that bring spiritual power. Immerse yourself in the scriptures. Pray daily for the Lord to give you strength beyond your own. At times, fast for special blessings.

Full obedience brings the complete power of the gospel into your life, including increased strength to overcome your weaknesses. This obedience includes actions you might not initially consider part of repentance, such as attending meetings, paying tithing, giving service, and forgiving others. The Lord promised, "He that repents and does the commandments of the Lord shall be forgiven" (D&C 1:32).

Additional references: Luke 15:11–32; 2 Nephi 9:19–24; Mosiah 4:1–3, 10–13; 26:30–31; D&C 18:10–16

*See also* Atonement of Jesus Christ; Baptism; Church Disciplinary Councils; Faith; Forgiveness; Plan of Salvation; Sin; Temptation

## Restoration of the Gospel

When Jesus Christ was on the earth, He established His Church among His followers. After His Crucifixion and the deaths of His Apostles, the fulness of the gospel was taken from the earth because of widespread apostasy (see "Apostasy," pages 13–14). Many men and women sought the fulness of gospel truth during the centuries of the Great Apostasy, but they were unable to find it. Although many preached with sincerity about the Savior and His teachings, none had the fulness of the truth or priesthood authority from God.

The Great Apostasy was a time of spiritual darkness, but we now live in a time when we can partake of "the light of the glorious gospel of Christ" (2 Corinthians 4:4; see also D&C 45:28). The fulness of the gospel has been restored, and the true Church of Jesus Christ is on the earth again. No other organization can compare to it. It is not the result of a reformation, with well-meaning men and women doing all in their power to bring about change. It is a restoration of the Church established by Jesus Christ. It is the work of Heavenly Father and His Beloved Son.

As a member of The Church of Jesus Christ of Latter-day Saints, you can receive blessings that were absent from the earth for almost 2,000 years. Through the ordinances of baptism and confirmation, you can receive the remission of your sins and enjoy the constant companionship of the Holy Ghost. You can live the gospel in its fulness and simplicity. You can gain an understanding of the nature of the Godhead, the Atonement of Jesus Christ, the purpose of life on earth, and the reality of life after death. You have the privilege of being guided by living prophets, who teach God's will in our day. Temple ordinances enable you to receive guidance and peace, prepare for eternal life, be sealed to your family for eternity, and provide saving ordinances for your deceased ancestors.

## Events of the Restoration

The following outline summarizes a few of the important events in the restoration of the gospel and the establishment of The Church of Jesus Christ of Latter-day Saints, which the

Lord has declared is "the only true and living church upon the face of the whole earth" (D&C 1:30).

*Early spring, 1820.* Seeking the true Church of Jesus Christ, 14-year-old Joseph Smith prayed in a grove of trees near his home in Palmyra, New York. In answer to his humble prayer, Heavenly Father and Jesus Christ visited him and told him that he must not join any of the churches on the earth at that time. (See Joseph Smith—History 1:11–19.) In the Church we refer to this experience as Joseph Smith's First Vision.

*September 21–22, 1823.* Joseph Smith was visited by an angel named Moroni. Moroni prophesied of coming events and told Joseph of the Book of Mormon record, written on plates of gold. The angel allowed Joseph to see the gold plates, which were buried in the nearby Hill Cumorah. (See Joseph Smith—History 1:27–53.)

*September 22, 1827.* Joseph Smith received the gold plates from Moroni at the Hill Cumorah after having met with Moroni on September 22 of each of the previous four years. (See Joseph Smith—History 1:53, 59.)

*May 15, 1829.* Having read about baptism for the remission of sins as they worked on the translation of the gold plates, Joseph Smith and his scribe Oliver Cowdery went to a secluded area to inquire of the Lord concerning the matter. There, on the banks of the Susquehanna River near Harmony, Pennsylvania, they received the answer to their prayer. John the Baptist, a resurrected being, came to them as "a messenger from heaven . . . in a cloud of light." He conferred upon them the Aaronic Priesthood. Then, in obedience to his instructions, Joseph and Oliver baptized each other and ordained each other to the Aaronic Priesthood. (See Joseph Smith—History 1:68–72; see also D&C 13.)

*May 1829.* The ancient Apostles Peter, James, and John conferred the Melchizedek Priesthood upon Joseph Smith and Oliver Cowdery. (See D&C 128:20.)

*June 1829.* Guided "by the gift and power of God" (D&C 135:3), the Prophet Joseph Smith completed the translation of the Book of Mormon.

*March 26, 1830.* The first printed copies of the Book of Mormon became available in Palmyra, New York.

*April 6, 1830.* The Church was organized in Fayette Township, New York, beginning with six members.

*March 27, 1836.* The Kirtland Temple, the first temple built in this dispensation, was dedicated. The Prophet Joseph Smith offered the dedicatory prayer, which had been given to him by revelation. (See D&C 109.)

*April 3, 1836.* The Savior appeared to Joseph Smith and Oliver Cowdery in the Kirtland Temple. Moses, Elias, and Elijah also appeared and gave priesthood keys to Joseph and Oliver. Elijah brought the keys of the sealing power, which make it possible for families to be sealed together forever. (See D&C 110.)

The Destiny of the Church

The Old Testament prophet Daniel prophesied that God would "set up a kingdom" that would "never be destroyed" and would "stand for ever" (Daniel 2:44). In making this prophecy, he spoke of The Church of Jesus Christ of Latter-day Saints, the kingdom of God on the earth today. From the day the Church was organized with six members, it has grown and flourished, and it will continue to progress until it has "filled the whole earth" (Daniel 2:35; see also D&C 65:2). Hundreds of thousands of people are baptized every year. The Book of Mormon is being translated in many languages. Temples are being built throughout the world. With Jesus Christ at the head of the Church, living prophets will guide the Church's progress until the earth is prepared for the Savior's Second Coming.

The Prophet Joseph Smith spoke of the blessings of the Restoration: "Now, what do we hear in the gospel which we have received? A voice of gladness! A voice of mercy from heaven; and a voice of truth out of the earth; glad tidings for the dead; a voice of gladness for the living and the dead; glad tidings of great joy" (D&C 128:19).

Additional references: Isaiah 2:1–3; 29:13–14; Acts 3:19–21; Revelation 14:6–7; 2 Nephi 3:3–15; D&C 128:19–21; 133:36–39, 57–58; Joseph Smith—History

*See also* Apostasy; Joseph Smith; Revelation; Second Coming of Jesus Christ

## Resurrection

Because of the Fall of Adam and Eve, we are subject to physical death, which is the separation of the spirit from the body. Through the Atonement of Jesus Christ, all people will be resurrected—saved from physical death (see 1 Corinthians 15:22). Resurrection is the reuniting of the spirit with the body in a perfect, immortal state, no longer subject to disease or death (see Alma 11:42–45).

The Savior was the first person on this earth to be resurrected. The New Testament contains several accounts testifying that He rose from the tomb (see Matthew 28:1–8; Mark 16:1–14; Luke 24:1–48; John 20:1–29; 1 Corinthians 15:1–8; 2 Peter 1:16–17).

When the resurrected Lord appeared to His Apostles, He helped them understand that He had a body of flesh and bones. He said, "Behold my hands and my feet, that it is I myself: handle me, and see; for a spirit hath not flesh and bones, as ye see me have" (Luke 24:39). He also appeared to the Nephites after His Resurrection (see 3 Nephi 11:10–17).

At the time of the resurrection, we will "be judged according to [our] works. . . . We shall be brought to stand before God, knowing even as we know now, and have a bright recollection of all our guilt" (Alma 11:41, 43). The eternal glory we receive will depend on our faithfulness. Although all people will be resurrected, only those who have come unto Christ and partaken of the fulness of His gospel will inherit exaltation in the celestial kingdom.

An understanding and testimony of the resurrection can give you hope and perspective as you experience the challenges, trials, and triumphs of life. You can find comfort in the assurance that the Savior lives and that through His Atonement, "he breaketh the bands of death, that the grave shall have no victory, and that the sting of death should be swallowed up in the hopes of glory" (Alma 22:14).

Additional references: Isaiah 25:8; 26:19; John 5:25–29; 11:25–26; 1 Corinthians 15; Enos 1:27; Alma 40:23–26; 41; Mormon 9:12–14; D&C 88:15–16; 93:33–34; Moses 1:39

*See also* Atonement of Jesus Christ; Death, Physical; Kingdoms of Glory; Plan of Salvation; Salvation; Soul

## Revelation

Revelation is communication from God to His children. This guidance comes through various channels according to the needs and circumstances of individuals, families, and the Church as a whole.

When the Lord reveals His will to the Church, He speaks through His prophet. The scriptures contain many such revelations—the word of the Lord through ancient and latter-day prophets. Today the Lord continues to guide the Church by revealing His will to His chosen servants.

Prophets are not the only people who can receive revelation. According to your faithfulness, you can receive revelation to help you with your specific needs, responsibilities, and questions and to help you strengthen your testimony.

## Preparing to Receive Revelation through the Holy Ghost

The scriptures tell of different types of revelation, such as visions, dreams, and visitations by angels. Through such channels, the Lord has restored His gospel in the latter days and revealed truths concerning such doctrines as premortal existence, the redemption of the dead, and the three kingdoms of glory. However, most revelations to leaders and members of the Church come through the whisperings of the Holy Ghost.

Quiet spiritual promptings may not seem as spectacular as visions or angelic visitations, but they are more powerful and lasting and life changing. The witness of the Holy Ghost makes an impression on the soul that is more significant than anything you can see or hear. Through such revelations, you will receive lasting strength to stay true to the gospel and help others do the same.

The following counsel will help you prepare to receive promptings from the Holy Ghost:

*Pray for guidance.* The Lord said, "Ask, and it shall be given you; seek, and ye shall find; knock, and it shall be opened unto you: for every one that asketh receiveth; and he that seeketh findeth; and to him that knocketh it shall be opened" (Matthew 7:7–8). In order to find and receive, you must seek and ask. If you do not knock—praying to your Heavenly Father for guidance—the door of revelation will not be opened to you. But if you approach your Father in humble prayer, you can eventually "receive revelation upon revelation, knowledge upon knowledge, that thou mayest know the mysteries and peaceable things—that which bringeth joy, that which bringeth life eternal" (D&C 42:61).

*Be reverent.* Reverence is profound respect and love. When you are reverent and peaceful, you invite revelation. Even when everything around you is in commotion, you can have a reverent attitude and be prepared to receive guidance from the Lord.

*Be humble.* Humility is closely related to reverence. When you are humble, you recognize your dependence on the Lord. The prophet Mormon taught, "Because of meekness and lowliness of heart cometh the visitation of the Holy Ghost, which Comforter filleth with hope and perfect love" (Moroni 8:26).

*Keep the commandments.* When you keep the commandments, you are prepared to receive, recognize, and follow the promptings of the Holy Ghost. The Lord promised, "Unto him that keepeth my commandments I will give the mysteries of my kingdom, and the same shall be in him a well of living water, springing up unto everlasting life" (D&C 63:23).

*Partake of the sacrament worthily.* The sacramental prayers teach how to receive the constant companionship of the Holy Spirit. When you partake of the sacrament, you witness to God that you are willing to take upon yourself the name of His Son and that you will always remember Him and keep His commandments. Heavenly Father promises that when you keep these covenants, you will always have the Spirit to be with you. (See D&C 20:77, 79.)

*Study the scriptures every day.* As you diligently study the scriptures, you learn from the examples of men and women whose lives have been blessed as they have followed the Lord's revealed will. You also become more receptive to the Holy Ghost in your own life. As you read and ponder, you may receive revelation about how a certain scripture passage applies to you or about anything else the Lord desires to communicate to you. Because scripture reading can help you receive personal revelation, you should study the scriptures every day.

*Take time to ponder.* When you take time to ponder the truths of the gospel, you open your mind and heart to the guiding influence of the Holy Ghost (see 1 Nephi 11:1; D&C 76:19; 138:1–11). Pondering takes your thoughts from the trivial things of the world and brings you closer to the Spirit.

142

*When seeking specific guidance, study the matter out in your mind.* At times the Lord's communication will come only after you have studied a matter out in your own mind. The Lord explained this process to Oliver Cowdery, who served as Joseph Smith's scribe for much of the translation of the Book of Mormon. Through the Prophet Joseph Smith, the Lord spoke to Oliver Cowdery, explaining why Oliver had not been able to translate the Book of Mormon even though he had been given the gift to translate: "Behold, you have not understood; you have supposed that I would give it unto you, when you took no thought save it was to ask me. But, behold, I say unto you, that you must study it out in your mind; then you must ask me if it be right, and if it is right I will cause that your bosom shall burn within you; therefore, you shall feel that it is right" (D&C 9:7–8).

*Patiently seek God's will.* God reveals Himself "in his own time, and in his own way, and according to his own will" (see D&C 88:63–68). Revelation will probably come to you "line upon line, precept upon precept, here a little and there a little" (2 Nephi 28:30; see also Isaiah 28:10; D&C 98:12). Do not try to force spiritual things. Revelation does not come that way. Be patient and trust in the Lord's timing.

Recognizing the Promptings of the Holy Ghost

Amid the many noises and messengers in the world today, you must learn to recognize the whisperings of the Holy Ghost. Following are some of the principal ways the Holy Ghost communicates with us:

*He speaks to the mind and heart in a still, small voice.* The Lord taught: "I will tell you in your mind and in your heart, by the Holy Ghost, which shall come upon you and which shall dwell in your heart. Now, behold, this is the spirit of revelation" (D&C 8:2–3). Sometimes the Holy Ghost will help you understand a gospel truth or give you a prompting that "seems to occupy [your] mind, and press itself upon [your] feelings" (D&C 128:1). Although such revelation can have a powerful effect on you, it almost always comes quietly, as a "still small voice" (see 1 Kings 19:9–12; Helaman 5:30; D&C 85:6).

*He prompts us through our feelings.* Although we often describe communication from the Spirit as a voice, that voice is one that we feel more than we hear. And while we speak of "listening" to the whisperings of the Holy Ghost, we often describe a spiritual prompting by saying, "I had a feeling . . ." The Lord's counsel to Oliver Cowdery in section 9 of the Doctrine and Covenants, which is discussed on page 143, teaches this principle. However, this counsel is sometimes misunderstood. Upon reading that passage, some members of the Church become confused, fearing that they have never received a prompting from the Holy Ghost because they have never felt a burning in their bosom. Note the Lord's final words in Doctrine and Covenants 9:8: "Therefore, you shall feel that it is right." The burning described in this scripture passage signifies a feeling of comfort and serenity, not necessarily a sensation of heat. As you continue to seek and follow the Lord's will in your life, you will come to recognize how the Holy Ghost influences you personally.

*He brings peace.* The Holy Ghost is often called the Comforter (see John 14:26; D&C 39:6). As He reveals the will of the Lord to you, He will "speak peace to your mind" (D&C 6:23). The peace He gives cannot be counterfeited by worldly influences or false teachings. It is the peace the Savior promised when He assured His disciples that He would send the Comforter: "Peace I leave with you, my peace I give unto you: not as the world giveth, give I unto you. Let not your heart be troubled, neither let it be afraid" (John 14:27).

Additional references: Amos 3:7; Matthew 16:13–18; 1 Corinthians 2:9–14; 12:3; Revelation 19:10; Alma 5:43–48; 17:2–3; D&C 76:5–10; 121:26–33; Articles of Faith 1:7, 9

*See also* Faith; Holy Ghost; Prayer; Reverence; Scriptures; Spiritual Gifts

## Reverence

Reverence is profound respect and love. When you have a reverent attitude toward God, you honor Him, express your gratitude to Him, and obey His commandments.

You should be reverent in your behavior as well as your attitude. Reverent behavior includes prayer, scripture study, fasting, and payment of tithes and offerings. It includes wearing modest clothing and using clean, wholesome language. The depth of your reverence is evident in your choice of music and other entertainment, in the way you speak of sacred subjects, and in the way you dress and act when you attend church and the temple. You show your reverence for the Lord when you serve other people and treat them with kindness and respect.

As you become more reverent, you will notice a quiet transformation in your life. The Lord will pour out His Spirit more abundantly on you. You will be less troubled and confused. You will be able to receive revelation to help you solve personal and family problems.

Just as reverence brings you closer to God, irreverence suits the purposes of the adversary. Satan will tempt you to follow the world's trend to more noise, excitement, and contention and to less restraint and quiet dignity. Like a commander mounting a military invasion, he will try to jam the channels of communication between you and the Lord. Beware of such tactics, and strive to be reverent in all you do.

Additional references: Leviticus 26:2; Psalm 89:5–7; Hebrews 12:28; D&C 59:21; 63:61–62, 64; 109:21

*See also* Faith; Gratitude; Modesty; Prayer; Revelation; Worship

## Sabbath

The Sabbath is the Lord's day, set apart each week for rest and worship. In Old Testament times, God's covenant people observed the Sabbath on the seventh day of the week because God rested on the seventh day when He had created the earth. The Lord emphasized the importance of Sabbath observance in the Ten Commandments:

"Remember the sabbath day, to keep it holy.

"Six days shalt thou labour, and do all thy work:

"But the seventh day is the sabbath of the Lord thy God: in it thou shalt not do any work, thou, nor thy son, nor thy daughter, thy manservant, nor thy maidservant, nor thy cattle, nor thy stranger that is within thy gates:

"For in six days the Lord made heaven and earth, the sea, and all that in them is, and rested the seventh day: wherefore the Lord blessed the sabbath day, and hallowed it" (Exodus 20:8–11).

After the Resurrection of Jesus Christ, which occurred on the first day of the week, the Lord's disciples began observing the Sabbath on the first day of the week, Sunday (see Acts 20:7).

In the latter days, the Lord has commanded us to continue observing the Sabbath. He has promised that if we obey this commandment, we will receive "the fulness of the earth" (see D&C 59:16–20).

Because the Sabbath is a holy day, it should be reserved for worthy and holy activities. Abstaining from work and recreation is not enough. In fact, if we merely lounge about doing nothing on the Sabbath, we fail to keep the day holy. In a revelation given to Joseph Smith in 1831, the Lord commanded: "That thou mayest more fully keep thyself unspotted from the world, thou shalt go to the house of prayer and offer up thy sacraments upon my holy day; for verily this is a day appointed unto you to rest from your labors, and to pay thy devotions unto the Most High" (D&C 59:9–10). In harmony with this revelation, we attend sacrament meeting each week. Other Sabbath-day activities may include praying, meditating, studying the scriptures and the teachings of latter-day prophets, writing letters to family members and friends, reading wholesome material, visiting the sick and distressed, and attending other Church meetings.

Additional references: Exodus 31:16–17; Mosiah 18:23; D&C 59:11–14; 68:29

*See also* Reverence; Sacrament; Worship

## Sacrament

On the night before His Crucifixion, Jesus Christ met with His Apostles and instituted the sacrament. "He took bread, and gave thanks, and brake it, and gave unto them, saying, This is my body which is given for you: this do in remembrance of me. Likewise also the cup after supper, saying, This cup is the new testament in my blood, which is shed for you" (Luke 22:19–20). After His Resurrection, He instituted the sacrament among the Nephites (see 3 Nephi 18:1–11).

Today we partake of bread and water in remembrance of Jesus Christ's atoning sacrifice. This ordinance is an essential part of our worship and our spiritual development. The more we ponder its significance, the more sacred it becomes to us.

### Remembering the Savior and His Atonement

The sacrament provides an opportunity for you to remember with gratitude the life, ministry, and Atonement of the Son of God.

With broken bread, you remember His body. You can be mindful of His physical suffering—especially His suffering on the cross. You can remember that through His mercy and grace, all people will be resurrected and given the opportunity for eternal life with God.

With a small cup of water, you can remember that the Savior shed His blood in intense spiritual suffering and anguish, beginning in the Garden of Gethsemane. There He said, "My soul is exceeding sorrowful, even unto death" (Matthew 26:38). Submitting to the will of the Father, He suffered more than we can comprehend: "Blood [came] from every pore, so great [was] his anguish for the wickedness and the abominations of his people" (Mosiah 3:7). You can remember that through the shedding of His blood, Jesus

147

Christ saved you and all other people from what the scriptures call the "original guilt" of Adam's transgression (Moses 6:54). You can remember that He also suffered for the sins, sorrows, and pains of all Heavenly Father's children, providing remission of sins for those who repent and live the gospel (see 2 Nephi 9:21–23).

### Renewing Covenants and Promised Blessings

When you partake of the sacrament, you witness to God that your remembrance of His Son will extend beyond the short time of that sacred ordinance. You promise to remember Him always. You witness that you are willing to take upon yourself the name of Jesus Christ and that you will keep His commandments. In partaking of the sacrament and making these commitments, you renew your baptismal covenant (see Mosiah 18:8–10; D&C 20:37).

You receive great blessings when you keep the baptismal covenant. As you renew it, the Lord renews the promised remission of your sins. Cleansed from sin, you are able to "always have his Spirit to be with [you]" (D&C 20:77). The Spirit's constant companionship is one of the greatest gifts you can receive in mortality. The Spirit will guide you in the paths of righteousness and peace, leading you to eternal life with your Father in Heaven and Jesus Christ.

### Partaking Worthily

In preparation for the sacrament each week, take time to examine your life and repent of your sins. You do not need to be perfect in order to partake of the sacrament, but you should have a spirit of humility and repentance in your heart. Every week you should prepare for that sacred ordinance with a broken heart and a contrite spirit (see 3 Nephi 9:20).

If you approach the sacrament with the reverence and solemnity it deserves, it becomes a weekly opportunity for introspection, repentance, and rededication—a source of strength and a constant reminder of the Savior's Atonement.

Additional references: 1 Corinthians 11:23–29; Moroni 4–5; D&C 20:75–79; 27:2

*See also* Atonement of Jesus Christ; Covenant

## Sacrament Meeting (*See* Sabbath; Sacrament; Sacrifice)

## Sacrifice

To sacrifice is to give up something we value for the sake of something of greater worth. As Latter-day Saints, we have the opportunity to sacrifice worldly things for the Lord and His kingdom. Members of The Church of Jesus Christ of Latter-day Saints should be willing to make any sacrifice required by the Lord. If we were not required to make sacrifices, we would never be able to develop the faith necessary for eternal salvation.

The Atonement of Jesus Christ is the great and eternal sacrifice at the center of the gospel (see Alma 34:8–16). Before the Savior carried out the Atonement, His covenant people sacrificed animals as a symbol of His sacrifice. This practice helped them look ahead to the Atonement (see Moses 5:4–8). The command to offer animal sacrifices ended with the death of Jesus Christ. In the Church today, we partake of the sacrament in remembrance of the Savior's atoning sacrifice.

In addition to remembering the atoning sacrifice of Jesus Christ, we are to offer our own sacrifice: a broken heart and a contrite spirit. The Savior said: "Ye shall offer up unto me no more the shedding of blood; yea, your sacrifices and your burnt offerings shall be done away. . . . And ye shall offer for a sacrifice unto me a broken heart and a contrite spirit. And whoso cometh unto me with a broken heart and a contrite spirit, him will I baptize with fire and with the Holy Ghost" (3 Nephi 9:19–20).

To have a broken heart and a contrite spirit is to be humble and receptive to the will of God and to the counsel of those He has called to lead His Church. It also means to feel deep sorrow for sin and a sincere desire to repent. The prophet Lehi emphasized the importance of offering this sacrifice: "Behold, [Christ] offereth himself a sacrifice for sin, to answer the ends of the law, unto all those who have a broken heart and a contrite spirit; and unto none else can the ends of the law be answered" (2 Nephi 2:7). If we do not offer the sacrifice of a broken heart and a contrite spirit, we cannot fully receive the blessings that come through the Atonement.

If you are willing to sacrifice as the Lord has commanded, you will be accepted by Him. He taught: "All . . . who know their hearts are honest, and are broken, and their spirits contrite, and are willing to observe their covenants by sacrifice—yea, every sacrifice which I, the Lord, shall command—they are accepted of me" (D&C 97:8). With an eternal perspective, you can see that giving up the things of the world is really no sacrifice at all. The blessings you receive are greater than anything you ever give up.

Additional references: Matthew 19:16–22; D&C 59:8

*See also* Atonement of Jesus Christ; Love; Obedience; Repentance; Sacrament; Service

## Salvation

In your conversations with other Christians, you may sometimes be asked, "Have you been saved?" Those who ask this question usually refer to the act of sincerely confessing, or declaring, that you have accepted Jesus Christ as your personal Lord and Savior. In asking the question, they show their faith in the following words, written by the Apostle Paul:

"If thou shalt confess with thy mouth the Lord Jesus, and shalt believe in thine heart that God hath raised him from the dead, thou shalt be saved. For with the heart man believeth unto righteousness; and with the mouth confession is made unto salvation" (Romans 10:9–10).

Answering the Question "Have You Been Saved?"

In Romans 10:9–10, the words *saved* and *salvation* signify a covenant relationship with Jesus Christ. Through this covenant relationship, we are assured salvation from the eternal consequences of sin if we are obedient. Every faithful Latter-day Saint is saved according to this meaning. We have been converted to the restored gospel. Through the ordinance of baptism, we have entered into a covenant relationship with the Savior, taking His name upon ourselves. We renew our baptismal covenant by partaking of the sacrament.

Different Meanings of the Word *Salvation*

In the doctrine of The Church of Jesus Christ of Latter-day Saints, the terms *saved* and *salvation* have various meanings. According to these meanings, your answer to the question "Have you been saved?" will be either "Yes" or "Yes, but with conditions." The following explanations outline six different meanings of the word *salvation*.

*Salvation from Physical Death.* All people eventually die. But through the Atonement and Resurrection of Jesus Christ, all people will be resurrected—saved from physical death. Paul testified, "As in Adam all die, even so in Christ shall all be made alive" (1 Corinthians 15:22).

*Salvation from Sin.* To be cleansed from sin through the Savior's Atonement, you must exercise faith in Jesus Christ, repent, be baptized, and receive the gift of the Holy Ghost (see Acts 2:37–38). If you have been baptized and have received the Holy Ghost through the proper priesthood authority, you have already been conditionally saved from sin. You will not be completely saved from sin until you have finished your life on the earth, having faithfully endured to the end.

Note that you cannot be saved *in your sins;* you cannot receive unconditional salvation simply by declaring your belief in Christ with the understanding that you will inevitably commit sins throughout the rest of your life (see Alma 11:36–37). Through the grace of God, you can be saved *from your sins* (see Helaman 5:10–11). To receive this blessing, you must exercise faith in Jesus Christ, strive to keep the commandments, forsake sin, and renew your repentance and cleansing through the ordinance of the sacrament.

*Being Born Again.* You may sometimes be asked if you have been born again. The principle of spiritual rebirth appears frequently in the scriptures. The New Testament contains Jesus's teaching that we must be "born again" and that unless we are "born of water and of the Spirit, [we] cannot enter into the kingdom of God" (John 3:3, 5). This teaching is affirmed in the Book of Mormon: "All mankind, yea, men and women, all nations, kindreds, tongues and people, must be born again; yea, born of God, changed from their carnal and fallen state, to a state of righteousness, being redeemed of God, becoming his sons and daughters; and thus they become new creatures; and unless they do this, they can in nowise inherit the kingdom of God" (Mosiah 27:25–26).

This rebirth is a process that occurs after we have been baptized and have received the gift of the Holy Ghost. It comes as a result of our willingness "to enter into a covenant with our God to do his will, and to be obedient to his commandments in all things that he shall command us, all the remainder of our days" (Mosiah 5:5). Then our "hearts are changed through faith on his name; therefore, [we] are born of him" (Mosiah 5:7). If you have been baptized and have received the gift of the Holy Ghost, with the covenant to take upon yourself the name of Jesus Christ, you can say that you have been born again. And you can renew that rebirth each Sabbath when you partake of the sacrament.

*Salvation from Ignorance.* Many people live in a state of darkness, not knowing the light of the restored gospel. They are "only kept from the truth because they know not where to find it" (D&C 123:12). As a member of the Lord's Church, you are saved from this condition. You have a knowledge of God the Father, Jesus Christ, the purpose of life, the plan of salvation, and your eternal potential. You can live as a disciple of the Savior, who declared, "I am the light of the world: he that followeth me shall not walk in darkness, but shall have the light of life" (John 8:12).

*Salvation from the Second Death.* The scriptures sometimes speak of salvation from the second death. The second death is the final spiritual death—being cut off from righteousness and denied a place in any kingdom of glory (see Alma 12:32; D&C 88:24). This second death will not come until the Final Judgment, and it will come to very few (see D&C 76:31–37). Almost every person who has ever lived on the earth is assured salvation from the second death (see D&C 76:40–45).

*Eternal Life, or Exaltation.* In the scriptures, the words *saved* and *salvation* often refer to eternal life, or exaltation (see Abraham 2:11). Eternal life is to know Heavenly Father and Jesus Christ and dwell with Them forever—to inherit a place in the highest degree of the celestial kingdom (see John 17:3; D&C 131:1–4; 132:21–24). To receive this great gift, we must do more than repent of our sins and be baptized and confirmed by appropriate priesthood authority. Men must receive the Melchizedek Priesthood, and all Church members must make and keep sacred covenants in the temple, including eternal marriage.

If we use the word *salvation* to mean eternal life, none of us can say that we have been saved in mortality. That glorious gift can come only after the Final Judgment.

Additional references: Matthew 10:22; Mark 16:16; Ephesians 2:8–10; James 2:14–18; 2 Nephi 25:23, 26; Mosiah 5:8–15; 3 Nephi 9:21–22; Moroni 10:32–33; Articles of Faith 1:3

*See also* Atonement of Jesus Christ; Baptism; Eternal Life; Grace; Kingdoms of Glory; Plan of Salvation

## Satan

Satan, also called the adversary or the devil, is the enemy of righteousness and those who seek to follow God. He is a spirit son of God who was once an angel "in authority in the presence of God" (D&C 76:25; see also Isaiah 14:12; D&C 76:26–27). But in the premortal Council in Heaven, Lucifer, as Satan was then called, rebelled against Heavenly Father and the plan of salvation. In this rebellion against God, Satan "sought to destroy the agency of man" (Moses 4:3). He said: "I will redeem all mankind, that one soul shall not be lost, and surely I will do it; wherefore give me thine honor" (Moses 4:1).

Satan persuaded "a third part of the hosts of heaven" to turn away from the Father (D&C 29:36). As a result of this rebellion, Satan and his followers were cut off from God's presence and denied the blessing of receiving a physical body (see Revelation 12:9). They were also denied the opportunity to receive any inheritance in a kingdom of glory.

Heavenly Father allows Satan and Satan's followers to tempt us as part of our experience in mortality (see 2 Nephi 2:11–14; D&C 29:39). Because Satan "seeketh that all men might be miserable like unto himself" (2 Nephi 2:27), he and his followers try to lead us away from righteousness. He directs his most strenuous opposition at the most important aspects of Heavenly Father's plan of happiness. For example, he seeks to discredit the Savior and the priesthood, to cast doubt on the power of the Atonement, to counterfeit revelation, to distract us from the truth, and to contradict individual accountability. He attempts to undermine the family by confusing gender, promoting sexual relations outside of marriage, ridiculing marriage, and discouraging childbearing by married adults who would otherwise raise children in righteousness.

You do not have to give in to Satan's temptations. You have the power within you to choose good over evil, and you can always seek the Lord's help through prayer. (See "Temptation," pages 174–76.)

Additional references: Isaiah 14:12–17; 1 Nephi 15:23–24; 2 Nephi 2:16–18; Moroni 7:12; D&C 10:5; 29:36–40, 46–47; 76:25–29

*See also* Agency; Sin; Temptation

**Saved** (*See* Salvation)

## Scriptures

When holy men of God write or speak by the power of the Holy Ghost, their words "shall be scripture, shall be the will of the Lord, shall be the mind of the Lord, shall be the word of the Lord, shall be the voice of the Lord, and the power of God unto salvation" (D&C 68:4). The official, canonized scriptures of the Church, often called the standard works, are the Bible, the Book of Mormon, the Doctrine and Covenants, and the Pearl of Great Price. These books of scripture are described on pages 156–59.

Importance of Daily Scripture Study

The principal purpose of scriptures is to testify of Christ, helping us come unto Him and receive eternal life (see John 5:39; 20:31; 1 Nephi 6:4; Mosiah 13:33–35). The prophet Mormon testified:

"Whosoever will may lay hold upon the word of God, which is quick and powerful, which shall divide asunder all the cunning and the snares and the wiles of the devil, and lead the man of Christ in a strait and narrow course across that everlasting gulf of misery which is prepared to engulf the wicked—

"And land their souls, yea, their immortal souls, at the right hand of God in the kingdom of heaven, to sit down with Abraham, and Isaac, and with Jacob, and with all our holy fathers, to go no more out" (Helaman 3:29–30).

Latter-day prophets counsel us to study the scriptures every day, both individually and with our families. They encourage us, as Nephi encouraged his brethren, to liken the scriptures to ourselves, finding ways that the sacred accounts of old apply in our lives today (see 1 Nephi 19:23–24). They exhort us to "search the scriptures" (John 5:39) and "feast upon the words of Christ" (2 Nephi 32:3).

You will benefit greatly by following this counsel. Daily, meaningful scripture study helps you be receptive to the whisperings of the Holy Ghost. It builds your faith, fortifies you against temptation, and helps you draw near to your Heavenly Father and His Beloved Son.

Develop a plan for your personal study of the scriptures. Consider setting aside a certain amount of time each day to study the scriptures. During that time, read carefully, being attentive to the promptings of the Spirit. Ask your Heavenly Father to help you know what He would have you learn and do.

Continue reading the scriptures, particularly the Book of Mormon, throughout your life. You will rediscover the treasures of the scriptures again and again, finding new meaning and application in them as you study them at different stages of life.

If you are married, set aside time each day to read the scriptures as a family. This effort may be difficult, but it will yield wonderful, eternal results. Under the guidance of the Spirit, plan scripture reading that will meet the needs of your family. Do not be afraid of reading the scriptures to small children. The language of those sacred records has power to touch even the very young.

## The Bible

The Bible is divided into two parts: the Old Testament and the New Testament. The Old Testament is a sacred record of God's dealings with His covenant people in the Holy Land. It includes the teachings of such prophets as Moses, Joshua,

Isaiah, Jeremiah, and Daniel. The New Testament records the birth, mortal ministry, and Atonement of the Savior. It concludes with the ministry of the Savior's disciples.

Because the Bible has been translated many times, it is printed in different versions. In English, the King James Version of the Bible is accepted as scripture by the Church.

In The Church of Jesus Christ of Latter-day Saints, we revere the Bible and its sacred teachings. We can receive strength and comfort from the biblical accounts of God's dealings with His people.

The Book of Mormon: Another Testament of Jesus Christ

The Book of Mormon came forth in this dispensation by the will of the Lord. It is a record of God's dealings with the people who lived in the ancient Americas. Prophets of the Lord engraved the original records on gold plates. The Lord declared that the Book of Mormon contains "the fulness of the gospel of Jesus Christ" (D&C 20:9; see also D&C 42:12).

On September 22, 1827, an angel named Moroni—the last Book of Mormon prophet—delivered these records to the Prophet Joseph Smith. By the gift and power of God, the Prophet Joseph translated the record into English. Since then, the Book of Mormon has been translated into many other languages.

The primary purpose of the Book of Mormon is to convince all people "that Jesus is the Christ, the Eternal God, manifesting himself unto all nations" (title page of the Book of Mormon). It teaches that all people "must come unto him, or they cannot be saved" (1 Nephi 13:40). Joseph Smith said that the Book of Mormon is "the keystone of our religion, and a man [will] get nearer to God by abiding by its precepts, than by any other book" (introduction to the Book of Mormon).

The Book of Mormon is another witness for the truths taught in the Bible. It also restores "plain and precious" truths that have been lost from the Bible through errors in translation or "taken away" in attempts to "pervert the right ways of the Lord" (see 1 Nephi 13:24–27, 38–41). The Bible and the Book of Mormon "shall grow together, unto the confounding of false doctrines and laying down of contentions, and establishing peace" (2 Nephi 3:12).

Near the end of the Book of Mormon, the prophet Moroni teaches us how we can know the book is true: "When ye shall receive these things, I would exhort you that ye would ask God, the Eternal Father, in the name of Christ, if these things are not true; and if ye shall ask with a sincere heart, with real intent, having faith in Christ, he will manifest the truth of it unto you, by the power of the Holy Ghost" (Moroni 10:4; see also verses 3 and 5).

## The Doctrine and Covenants

The Doctrine and Covenants contains revelations given to the Prophet Joseph Smith. It also includes a few revelations given to other latter-day prophets. This book of scripture is unique because it is not a translation of ancient documents. It is a collection of revelations given by the Lord to His chosen prophets in the latter days.

The Prophet Joseph Smith said that the Doctrine and Covenants is "the foundation of the Church in these last days, and a benefit to the world, showing that the keys of the mysteries of the kingdom of our Savior are again entrusted to man" (section heading for D&C 70).

## The Pearl of Great Price

The Pearl of Great Price contains the book of Moses, the book of Abraham, the Prophet Joseph Smith's inspired translation of Matthew chapter 24, and some writings of the Prophet Joseph.

The book of Moses is a small excerpt from Joseph Smith's inspired translation of the Bible. It is a more complete record of Moses's writings at the beginning of the book of Genesis in the Old Testament. It contains many doctrines and teachings that were lost from the Bible and gives additional information about the plan of salvation, the creation of the earth, and the Lord's dealings with Adam and Enoch.

The book of Abraham is a translation of ancient records written on papyrus that came into the possession of the Church in 1835. The Prophet Joseph Smith translated the records by revelation. This book contains truths about the premortal Council in Heaven, the creation of the earth, the nature of God, and the priesthood.

Joseph Smith—Matthew adds to our knowledge of the Savior's teachings about His Second Coming.

The writings of Joseph Smith in the Pearl of Great Price include:

- Joseph Smith—History, which is an excerpt from the Prophet's history of the Church. It is a narrative of the events leading to the restoration of the Church, including the First Vision, the visits of Moroni to the Prophet Joseph, the obtaining of the gold plates, and the restoration of the Aaronic Priesthood.

- The Articles of Faith, which the Prophet Joseph Smith wrote as basic statements of belief and doctrine.

Additional references: Romans 15:4; 2 Timothy 3:15–17; 2 Nephi 25:26; Alma 17:2–3; 3 Nephi 23:1–5; D&C 18:33–36; Articles of Faith 1:8

*See also* Prophets; Restoration of the Gospel; Revelation

## Second Coming of Jesus Christ

As Jesus Christ ascended into heaven at the completion of His mortal ministry, two angels declared to His Apostles, "This same Jesus, which is taken up from you into heaven, shall so come in like manner as ye have seen him go into heaven" (Acts 1:11). When the Savior comes again, He will come in power and glory to claim the earth as His kingdom.

His Second Coming will mark the beginning of the Millennium.

The Second Coming will be a fearful, mournful time for the wicked, but it will be a day of peace and triumph for the righteous. The Lord declared:

"They that are wise and have received the truth, and have taken the Holy Spirit for their guide, and have not been deceived—verily I say unto you, they shall not be hewn down and cast into the fire, but shall abide the day.

"And the earth shall be given unto them for an inheritance; and they shall multiply and wax strong, and their children shall grow up without sin unto salvation.

"For the Lord shall be in their midst, and his glory shall be upon them, and he will be their king and their lawgiver" (D&C 45:57–59).

The Lord has not revealed exactly when He will come again: "The hour and the day no man knoweth, neither the angels in heaven, nor shall they know until he comes" (D&C 49:7). But He has revealed to His prophets the events and signs that will precede His Second Coming. Among the prophesied events and signs are:

- Apostasy from gospel truth (see Matthew 24:9–12; 2 Thessalonians 2:1–3).

- The restoration of the gospel, including the restoration of the Church of Jesus Christ (see Acts 3:19–21; Revelation 14:6–7; D&C 45:28; 133:36).

- The restoration of priesthood keys (see Malachi 4:5–6; D&C 110:11–16).

- The coming forth of the Book of Mormon (see Isaiah 29:4–18; 3 Nephi 21:1–11).

- The preaching of the gospel throughout the world (see Matthew 24:14).

- A time of wickedness, war, and turmoil (see Matthew 24:6–7; 2 Timothy 3:1–7; D&C 29:17; 45:26–33; 88:91).

- Signs in heaven and on the earth (see Joel 2:30–31; Matthew 24:29–30; D&C 29:14–16; 45:39–42; 49:23; 88:87–90).

Do not concern yourself with the exact timing of the Savior's Second Coming. Instead, live so that you will be prepared whenever He comes. As you observe the calamities of these last days, remember that the righteous need not fear the Second Coming or the signs that precede it. The Savior's words to His Apostles apply to you: "Be not troubled, for, when all these things shall come to pass, ye may know that the promises which have been made unto you shall be fulfilled" (D&C 45:35).

Additional references: Luke 21:34–36; 2 Peter 3:10–14; D&C 133:42–52; Joseph Smith—Matthew

*See also* Millennium; Plan of Salvation; Signs

## Service

True disciples of Jesus Christ desire to serve those around them. The Savior said, "By this shall all men know that ye are my disciples, if ye have love one to another" (John 13:35).

When you were baptized, you covenanted to take the name of Jesus Christ upon yourself. The prophet Alma explained this covenant to a group of new converts who wanted to be baptized. He observed that their desire to "come into the fold of God" included a willingness to give meaningful service—to "bear one another's burdens, that they may be light," to "mourn with those that mourn," and to "comfort those that stand in need of comfort" (Mosiah 18:8–9).

As you strive to serve others, look to the Savior as your example. Even though He came to earth as the Son of God, He humbly served all those around Him. He declared, "I am among you as he that serveth" (Luke 22:27).

## Seventy

The Savior used a parable to teach the importance of service. In the parable, He returns to the earth in His glory and separates the righteous from the wicked. To the righteous He says: "Come, ye blessed of my Father, inherit the kingdom prepared for you from the foundation of the world: For I was an hungred, and ye gave me meat: I was thirsty, and ye gave me drink: I was a stranger, and ye took me in: naked, and ye clothed me: I was sick, and ye visited me: I was in prison, and ye came unto me" (Matthew 25:34–36).

The righteous, who are puzzled by this declaration, ask: "Lord, when saw we thee an hungred, and fed thee? or thirsty, and gave thee drink? When saw we thee a stranger, and took thee in? or naked, and clothed thee? Or when saw we thee sick, or in prison, and came unto thee?" (Matthew 25:37–39).

Then the Lord answers, "Inasmuch as ye have done it unto one of the least of these my brethren, ye have done it unto me" (Matthew 25:40).

The Savior invites you to give of yourself in the service of others. Your opportunities to do so are limitless. Each day, look for ways to gladden hearts, to say kind words, to perform labors for others that they cannot do for themselves, to share the gospel. Be receptive to the whisperings of the Spirit, prompting you to serve. You will find that the true key to happiness is to labor for the happiness of others.

Additional references: Matthew 22:35–40; 25:41–46; Luke 10:25–37; Galatians 5:13–14; Mosiah 2:17

*See also* Charity; Love

**Seventy** (*See* Church Administration)

**Sexual Immorality** (*See* Chastity)

## Signs

Signs are events or experiences that demonstrate the power of God. They are often miraculous. They identify and announce great events, such as the Savior's birth, death, and Second Coming. They remind us of covenants the Lord has made with us. Signs may also bear witness of a divine calling or indicate the Lord's disapproval.

Some people claim that they would believe in God or His work if they were able to receive a sign. But the Lord has said, "Faith cometh not by signs, but signs follow those that believe" (D&C 63:9). Such signs are given to those who are faithful and obedient in order to strengthen them in their faith.

Additional references: Matthew 12:38–39; Mark 13:22–27; Luke 2:8–17; Alma 30:43–52; Helaman 14; 3 Nephi 1:13–21; 8:2–25; Ether 12:6; D&C 63:7–12

*See also* Faith; Obedience; Second Coming of Jesus Christ

## Sin

When we willfully disobey God's commandments, we commit sin. We also commit sin when we fail to act righteously despite our knowledge of the truth (see James 4:17).

The Lord has said that He "cannot look upon sin with the least degree of allowance" (D&C 1:31). The result of sin is the withdrawal of the Holy Ghost and, in eternity, being unable to dwell in the presence of our Heavenly Father, for "no unclean thing can dwell with God" (1 Nephi 10:21).

Each of us has broken commandments or failed to act according to our knowledge of the truth. The Apostle John taught: "If we say that we have no sin, we deceive ourselves, and the truth is not in us. If we confess our sins, [Jesus Christ] is faithful and just to forgive us our sins, and to cleanse us from all unrighteousness" (1 John 1:8–9). Through the Atonement of Jesus Christ, we can repent and be forgiven of our sins.

Additional references: Romans 3:23; 6:23; Alma 5:41–42; 11:37; Helaman 5:10–11; D&C 82:1–3; 88:34–35

*See also* Atonement of Jesus Christ; Death, Spiritual; Forgiveness; Justice; Mercy; Obedience; Repentance; Temptation

## Smith, Joseph Jr. *(See* Joseph Smith)

## Soul

The term *soul* is used in two ways in the scriptures. First, a spirit that is united with a physical body, whether in mortality or after resurrection, is called a soul (see D&C 88:15–16). Second, our spirits are sometimes called souls (see Alma 40:15–18; Abraham 3:23).

*See also* Plan of Salvation; Resurrection; Spirit

## Spirit

You are a spirit child of Heavenly Father, and you existed as a spirit before you were born on the earth. During your life on the earth, your spirit is housed in your physical body, which was born of mortal parents.

From the scriptures, we learn about the nature of spirits. We learn that "all spirit is matter, but it is more fine or pure, and can only be discerned by purer eyes" (D&C 131:7). We read that "the spirit of man [is] in the likeness of his person, as also the spirit of the beast, and every other creature which God has created" (D&C 77:2; see also Ether 3:7–16).

The scriptures also teach that at the time of physical death, the spirit does not die. It separates from the body and lives in the postmortal spirit world. At the time of resurrection, the spirit is reunited with the body, "never to be divided; thus the whole becoming spiritual and immortal" (Alma 11:45).

Additional references: Romans 8:16–17; 2 Nephi 9:10–13; D&C 93:29, 33

*See also* Plan of Salvation; Resurrection; Soul

**Spirit of the Lord** (*See* Holy Ghost; Light of Christ)

**Spirit of Truth** (*See* Holy Ghost)

**Spirit Prison** (*See* Death, Physical; Hell; Paradise)

**Spiritual Death** (*See* Death, Spiritual)

## Spiritual Gifts

Spiritual gifts are blessings or abilities that are given by the power of the Holy Ghost. God gives at least one of these gifts to every faithful member of the Church. As you receive these gifts, they will strengthen and bless you individually and help you serve others. (See D&C 46:8–12.) The scriptures teach of many gifts of the Spirit:

- Knowledge "that Jesus Christ is the Son of God, and that he was crucified for the sins of the world" (D&C 46:13).
- The capacity to believe the words of those who testify of Jesus Christ (see D&C 46:14).
- Knowledge of "the differences of administration" (D&C 46:15; see also 1 Corinthians 12:5). This gift is used in administering and leading the Church.
- Knowledge of "the diversities of operations," which helps us discern whether a teaching or influence comes from God or from some other source (D&C 46:16; see also 1 Corinthians 12:6–7).
- The gift of "the word of wisdom" (1 Corinthians 12:8; D&C 46:17). This does not refer to the law we know as

the Word of Wisdom. Rather, it is the gift of wisdom—the ability to use knowledge in righteous ways.

- The gift of "the word of knowledge" (1 Corinthians 12:8; D&C 46:18).
- The ability to teach by the power of the Holy Ghost (see Moroni 10:9–10; see also D&C 46:18).
- The gift of faith (see 1 Corinthians 12:9; Moroni 10:11).
- The gift "to have faith to be healed" (D&C 46:19).
- The gift "to have faith to heal" (D&C 46:20; see also 1 Corinthians 12:9; Moroni 10:11).
- "The working of miracles" (1 Corinthians 12:10; D&C 46:21; see also Moroni 10:12).
- The gift of prophecy (see 1 Corinthians 12:10; Moroni 10:13; D&C 46:22). John the Beloved taught that "the testimony of Jesus is the spirit of prophecy" (Revelation 19:10).
- "The beholding of angels and ministering spirits" (Moroni 10:14).
- "Discerning of spirits" (1 Corinthians 12:10; D&C 46:23).
- The gift to speak in different languages, or tongues (see 1 Corinthians 12:10; Moroni 10:15; D&C 46:24).
- The gift of "the interpretation of tongues" (1 Corinthians 12:10; D&C 46:25; see also Moroni 10:16).

These spiritual gifts and others listed in the scriptures are only some examples of the many gifts of the Spirit. The Lord may bless you in other ways depending on your faithfulness and on your needs and the needs of those you serve. He has commanded us to work diligently so we can receive spiritual gifts:

"Beware lest ye are deceived; and that ye may not be deceived seek ye earnestly the best gifts, always remembering for what they are given;

"For verily I say unto you, they are given for the benefit of those who love me and keep all my commandments, and him that seeketh so to do; that all may be benefited that seek or that ask of me" (D&C 46:8–9; see also verse 26).

Additional references: 1 Corinthians 13; 14:1–33; Moroni 10:17–25; D&C 46:27–33; Articles of Faith 1:7

*See also* Holy Ghost; Revelation

**Stake** (*See* Church Administration)

**Standard Works** (*See* Scriptures)

**Sunday** (*See* Sabbath; Worship)

**Swearing** (*See* Profanity)

## Tattooing

Latter-day prophets strongly discourage the tattooing of the body. Those who disregard this counsel show a lack of respect for themselves and for God. The Apostle Paul taught of the significance of our bodies and the danger of purposefully defiling them: "Know ye not that ye are the temple of God, and that the Spirit of God dwelleth in you? If any man defile the temple of God, him shall God destroy; for the temple of God is holy, which temple ye are" (1 Corinthians 3:16–17).

If you have a tattoo, you wear a constant reminder of a mistake you have made. You might consider having it removed.

*See also* Body Piercing

**Tea** (*See* Word of Wisdom)

## Teaching the Gospel

The Lord has declared: "I give unto you a commandment that you shall teach one another the doctrine of the kingdom. Teach ye diligently and my grace shall attend you, that you may be instructed more perfectly in theory, in principle, in doctrine, in the law of the gospel, in all things that pertain unto the kingdom of God, that are expedient for you to understand" (D&C 88:77–78).

In giving this commandment, the Lord gives us a sacred responsibility. He also leads us to countless opportunities for meaningful service. Few experiences compare to the joy of helping others learn and live the gospel.

This commandment to teach applies to you, even if you do not currently have a formal calling as a teacher. You have teaching opportunities as a member of your family, as a home teacher or visiting teacher, and even as a coworker, neighbor, and friend. Sometimes you teach through words you have prepared to say. Sometimes you can take advantage of brief, unplanned moments in which you can share gospel truths. Most frequently you teach by example.

Teaching as the Savior Taught

In your efforts to teach the gospel, look to Jesus Christ as your example. Study accounts of His mortal ministry, and look for ways to teach as He taught. He showed genuine love and concern for those He served. He strengthened people individually, teaching gospel principles in a way that would help them with their unique needs. He awakened in some the desire to understand and live the gospel. At times He asked questions that would help them apply what they learned. He taught the saving truths of the gospel, helping His hearers understand what they needed to know, do, and be in order to receive the gift of eternal life.

As you follow the Savior's example, your teaching will nourish and uplift others, build their faith, and give them confidence to meet life's challenges. It will encourage them to forsake sin and obey the commandments. It will help them come to Christ and abide in His love.

## Teaching by the Spirit

The Lord said, "The Spirit shall be given unto you by the prayer of faith; and if ye receive not the Spirit ye shall not teach" (D&C 42:14). The Spirit, or the Holy Ghost, is a member of the Godhead. One purpose of the Spirit is to "manifest the truth . . . of all things" (Moroni 10:4–5). Only through the influence of the Spirit can gospel teaching be edifying and inspiring.

Your privilege as a gospel teacher is to be an instrument through whom the Holy Ghost can teach, testify, comfort, and inspire. As the prophet Nephi taught, "When a man speaketh by the power of the Holy Ghost the power of the Holy Ghost carrieth it unto the hearts of the children of men" (2 Nephi 33:1).

If you prepare spiritually, the Holy Ghost will help you know what to do and say in your teaching. You can prepare yourself by praying often, studying the scriptures, living the gospel, and being humble.

## Methods of Teaching

Your teaching will be most effective when you use a variety of appropriate methods. For example, you can share stories and examples to hold people's attention and show how gospel principles apply in daily life. You can use pictures and objects to strengthen others' understanding of scripture accounts and gospel principles. Through music, you and those you teach can invite the influence of the Holy Ghost and express feelings that may be hard to express in other ways. You can ask questions that encourage thoughtful learning and discussion and that lead to the appropriate sharing of personal experiences. With simple activities, you can help learners focus their attention.

When you consider using a specific teaching method, ask yourself the following questions: Will this method invite the influence of the Spirit? Does it match the sacredness of the principles I am teaching? Will it edify and strengthen those I teach?

Remember that as a gospel teacher, you represent the Lord. Ensure that all you do and say is reverent and consistent with His will.

For additional suggestions on gospel teaching, you may want to refer to *Teaching, No Greater Call* (36123); the *Teaching Guidebook* (34595); and "Gospel Teaching and Leadership," section 16 of the *Church Handbook of Instructions, Book 2: Priesthood and Auxiliary Leaders* (35903).

Additional references: Mosiah 18:19; Alma 1:26; 17:2–3; 31:5; D&C 11:21

**Telestial Kingdom** (*See* Kingdoms of Glory)

## Temples

Temples are literally houses of the Lord. They are holy places of worship where the Lord may visit. Only the home can compare with temples in sacredness.

Throughout history, the Lord has commanded His people to build temples. Today the Church is heeding the Lord's call to build temples all over the world, making temple blessings more available for a great number of our Heavenly Father's children.

### Ordinances for the Living

The principal purpose of temples is to provide the ordinances necessary for our exaltation in the celestial kingdom. Temple ordinances lead to the greatest blessings available through the Atonement of Jesus Christ. All we do in the Church—our meetings and activities, our missionary efforts, the lessons we teach and the hymns we sing—should point us to the Savior and the work we do in holy temples.

One ordinance we receive in the temple is the endowment. The word *endowment* means "gift," and the temple endowment truly is a gift from God. The ordinance consists of a series of instructions and includes covenants we make to live righteously and comply with the requirements of the gospel. The endowment helps us focus on the Savior, His role in our Heavenly Father's plan, and our commitment to follow Him.

Another temple ordinance is celestial marriage, in which husband and wife are sealed to one another for eternity. A sealing performed in the temple continues forever if the husband and wife are faithful to the covenants they make.

Children born to parents who have been sealed in the temple are born in the covenant. These children automatically become part of an eternal family. Children who are not born in the covenant can also become part of an eternal family once their natural or adoptive parents have been sealed to one another. The ordinance of sealing children to parents is performed in the temple.

If you have received temple ordinances, always remember the covenants you have made. Return to the temple as often as you can. If you are a father or mother, teach your children the significance of the temple. Help them prepare themselves to be worthy to enter the temple.

If you have not yet received temple ordinances, begin preparing yourself now. As circumstances allow, attend the temple to participate in baptisms and confirmations for the dead.

Ordinances for the Dead

People who have died without essential gospel ordinances may receive those ordinances through the work done in temples. You may do this work in behalf of your ancestors and others who have died. Acting for them, you can be baptized and confirmed, receive the endowment, and participate in the sealings of husband to wife and children to parents.

You should actively search for the records of your deceased ancestors so temple work can be performed for them.

For more information about temple work for the dead and family history work, see "Family History Work and Genealogy," pages 61–64.

Worthiness to Enter the Temple

To enter the temple, you must be worthy. You certify your worthiness in two interviews—one with a member of your bishopric or your branch president and another with a member of your stake presidency or the mission president. Your priesthood leaders will keep these interviews private and confidential. In each of the interviews, the priesthood leader will ask you about your personal conduct and worthiness. You will be asked about your testimony of Heavenly Father and the Atonement of Jesus Christ, and you will be asked whether you support the general and local leaders of the Church. You will be asked to confirm that you are morally clean and that you keep the Word of Wisdom, pay a full tithe, live in harmony with the teachings of the Church, and do not maintain any affiliation or sympathy with apostate groups.

If you give acceptable answers to the questions in the interviews and if you and your priesthood leaders are satisfied that you are worthy to enter the temple, you will receive a temple recommend. You and your priesthood leaders will sign the recommend, which will allow you to enter the temple for the next two years, as long as you remain worthy.

Temple recommend interviews offer a great opportunity for you to examine your worthiness and the pattern of your life. If anything is amiss in your life, arrange to speak with your bishop or branch president well in advance of your temple recommend interview. He will be able to help you prepare yourself to be worthy of a temple recommend.

## Temple Clothing

When you go to the temple, you should wear your best clothing, as you do when you attend church. When you are inside the temple, you exchange your clothing for the white clothing of the temple. This change of clothing takes place in a dressing room, where you use a locker and a private dressing space. In the temple, modesty is carefully maintained.

As you put your clothing in the locker, you can leave all your worldly distractions behind. Dressed in white, you can feel a oneness and a sense of equality with others in the temple, for everyone around you is similarly dressed.

## Wearing the Temple Garment

Once you are endowed, you have the blessing of wearing the temple garment throughout your life. You are obligated to wear it according to the instructions given in the endowment. Remember that the blessings that are related to this sacred privilege depend on your worthiness and your faithfulness in keeping temple covenants.

The garment provides a constant reminder of the covenants you have made in the temple. You should treat it with respect at all times. You should not expose it to the view of those who do not understand its significance, and you should not adjust it to accommodate different styles of clothing. When you wear it properly, it provides protection against temptation and evil. Wearing the garment is an outward expression of an inward commitment to follow the Savior.

## Blessings from Attending the Temple

In addition to being a place where sacred priesthood ordinances are performed, the temple is a place of peace and revelation. When you are troubled or when crucial decisions weigh heavily on your mind, you may take your cares to the temple. There you can receive spiritual guidance.

Sometimes you may feel that you cannot think clearly because your mind is so burdened with problems and the many things clamoring for attention. In the temple, the dust of these distractions can settle, the fog and haze can lift, and you can understand things that you have not understood before. You can find new ways to deal with the challenges you face.

The Lord will bless you as you attend to the sacred ordinance work in the temple. And the blessings He gives you will not be limited to your time in the temple. He will bless you in all aspects of your life. Your labors in the temple will strengthen you and refine you spiritually.

Additional references: Isaiah 2:1–3; D&C 88:119; 109–110; 124:39–41

*See also* Covenant; Family History Work and Genealogy; Marriage; Ordinances; Plan of Salvation

## Temptation

As the Apostle Paul prophesied, the last days are "perilous times" (2 Timothy 3:1). The influence of the adversary is widespread and seductive. But you can defeat Satan and overcome his temptations. Heavenly Father has given you the gift of agency—the power to choose good over evil. You can "humble [yourself] before the Lord, and call on his holy name, and watch and pray continually, that [you] may not be tempted above that which [you] can bear" (Alma 13:28). As you willingly obey the commandments, your Heavenly Father will strengthen you to withstand temptation.

The following counsel will help you overcome temptation:

*Center your life on the Savior.* The prophet Helaman counseled his sons, "Remember, remember that it is upon the rock of our Redeemer, who is Christ, the Son of God, that ye must build your foundation; that when the devil shall send forth his mighty winds, yea, his shafts in the whirlwind, yea, when all his hail and his mighty storm shall beat upon you, it shall have no power over you to drag you down to the gulf of misery and endless wo, because of the rock upon which ye are built, which is a sure foundation, a foundation whereon if men build they cannot fall" (Helaman 5:12).

*Pray for strength.* When the resurrected Savior came to the Nephites, He taught the multitude: "Ye must watch and pray always lest ye enter into temptation; for Satan desireth to have you, that he may sift you as wheat. Therefore ye must always pray unto the Father in my name" (3 Nephi 18:18–19). In the latter days He has given similar counsel: "Pray always, that you may come off conqueror; yea, that you may conquer Satan, and that you may escape the hands of the servants of Satan that do uphold his work" (D&C 10:5).

*Study the scriptures daily.* As you study gospel truths and apply them in your life, the Lord will bless you with power to withstand temptation. Nephi taught, "Whoso would hearken unto the word of God, and would hold fast unto it, they would never perish; neither could the temptations and the fiery darts of the adversary overpower them unto blindness, to lead them away to destruction" (1 Nephi 15:24; see also Helaman 3:29–30).

*Fill your life with goodness.* You have so much good to choose from that you do not need to partake of evil. When you fill your life with goodness, you leave no room for anything else.

*Avoid tempting places and situations.* You cannot avoid temptation completely, but you can avoid places or situations where you are likely to be tempted. You can also avoid inappropriate material in magazines, books, television, movies, and music and on the Internet.

*Strive to influence others for good.* Just before He suffered in the Garden of Gethsemane, the Savior prayed for His disciples: "They are not of the world, even as I am not of the world. I pray not that thou shouldest take them out of the world, but that thou shouldest keep them from the evil. They are not of the world, even as I am not of the world. Sanctify them through thy truth: thy word is truth. As thou hast sent me into the world, even so have I also sent them into the world" (John 17:14–18). As a latter-day disciple of Jesus Christ, you can be in the world but "not of the world." In addition to avoiding temptation yourself, you can influence others to live good and wholesome lives. You can set a righteous example, be a good friend, participate in community service, and, as appropriate, let your voice be heard in defense of moral values.

*Never hesitate in your decisions to withstand temptation.* Strive to follow the example of the Savior, who "suffered temptations but gave no heed unto them" (D&C 20:22). When Satan tempted Jesus in the wilderness, the Lord never wavered. His answer was quick and firm: "Get thee behind me, Satan" (Luke 4:8). Through your righteous thoughts, words, and actions, you can answer the temptations of the adversary with the same conviction. "Resist the devil, and he will flee from you. Draw nigh to God, and he will draw nigh to you" (James 4:7–8).

Additional references: Romans 12:21; Ephesians 6:11–17; James 1:12, footnote *b*; D&C 23:1; 31:12; Moses 1:12–22

*See also* Agency; Conscience; Fasting and Fast Offerings; Holy Ghost; Light of Christ; Repentance; Satan

## Ten Commandments

The Ten Commandments are eternal gospel principles that are necessary for our exaltation. The Lord revealed them to Moses in ancient times (see Exodus 20:1–17), and He has restated them in latter-day revelations (see D&C 42:18–29; 59:5–13; 63:61–62). The Ten Commandments are a vital part of the gospel. Obedience to these commandments paves the way for obedience to other gospel principles.

The following review of the Ten Commandments includes brief explanations of how they continue to apply in our lives today:

1. "Thou shalt have no other gods before me" (Exodus 20:3). We should do "all things with an eye single to the glory of God" (D&C 82:19). We should love and serve the Lord with all our heart, might, mind, and strength (see Deuteronomy 6:5; D&C 59:5).

2. "Thou shalt not make unto thee any graven image" (Exodus 20:4). In this commandment, the Lord condemns the worship of idols. Idolatry may take many forms. Some people do not bow before graven images or statues but instead replace the living God with other idols, such as money, material possessions, ideas, or prestige. In their lives, "their treasure is their god"—a god that "shall perish with them" (2 Nephi 9:30).

3. "Thou shalt not take the name of the Lord thy God in vain" (Exodus 20:7). For an explanation of this commandment, see "Profanity," pages 128–29.

4. "Remember the sabbath day, to keep it holy" (Exodus 20:8). For an explanation of this commandment, see "Sabbath," pages 145–47.

5. "Honour thy father and thy mother" (Exodus 20:12). This is a commandment that remains binding even when we are grown. We should always find ways to honor our parents.

6. "Thou shalt not kill" (Exodus 20:13). For an explanation of how this commandment applies to those who are required to go to war, see "War," pages 183–84.

7. "Thou shalt not commit adultery" (Exodus 20:14). In a latter-day revelation, the Lord condemned not only adultery, but "anything like unto it" (D&C 59:6). Fornication, homosexuality, and other sexual sins are violations of the seventh commandment. For additional explanation, see "Chastity," pages 29–33.

8. "Thou shalt not steal" (Exodus 20:15). Stealing is a form of dishonesty. For an explanation of honesty, see page 84.

9. "Thou shalt not bear false witness against thy neighbour" (Exodus 20:16). Bearing false witness is another form of dishonesty. For an explanation of honesty, see page 84.

10. "Thou shalt not covet" (Exodus 20:17). Coveting, or envying something that belongs to another, is damaging to the soul. It can consume our thoughts and plague us with constant unhappiness and dissatisfaction. It often leads to other sins and to financial indebtedness.

Although most of the Ten Commandments list things we *should not* do, they also represent things we *should* do. The Savior summarized the Ten Commandments in two principles—love for the Lord and love for our fellow men:

"Thou shalt love the Lord thy God with all thy heart, and with all thy soul, and with all thy mind.

"This is the first and great commandment.

"And the second is like unto it, Thou shalt love thy neighbour as thyself" (Matthew 22:37–39).

Additional references: Mosiah 12:33–36; 13:11–24

*See also* Agency; Chastity; Honesty; Obedience; Profanity; Reverence; Sabbath; War; Worship

## Terrestrial Kingdom (*See* Kingdoms of Glory)

## Testimony

A testimony is a spiritual witness given by the Holy Ghost. The foundation of a testimony is the knowledge that Heavenly Father lives and loves us; that Jesus Christ lives, that He is the Son of God, and that He carried out the infinite Atonement; that Joseph Smith is the prophet of God who was called to restore the gospel; that we are led by a living prophet today; and that The Church of Jesus Christ of Latter-day Saints is the Savior's true Church on the earth. With this foundation, a testimony grows to include all principles of the gospel.

## Obtaining and Strengthening a Testimony

As a member of The Church of Jesus Christ of Latter-day Saints, you have the sacred opportunity and responsibility to obtain your own testimony. Having obtained a testimony, you have a duty to nurture it throughout your life. Your happiness in this life and throughout eternity depends largely on whether you are "valiant in the testimony of Jesus" (D&C 76:79; see also verses 51, 74, 101). As you work at this process, remember the following principles:

*The quest for a testimony begins with a righteous, sincere desire.* Your Heavenly Father will bless you according to the righteous desires of your heart and your efforts to do His will. Speaking to a group of people who did not yet have testimonies of the gospel, Alma taught: "If ye will awake and arouse your faculties, even to an experiment upon my words, and exercise a particle of faith, yea, even if ye can no more than desire to believe, let this desire work in you, even until ye believe in a manner that ye can give place for a portion of my words" (Alma 32:27).

*Testimony comes through the quiet influence of the Holy Ghost.* The results of a testimony can be miraculous and life changing, but the gift of testimony usually comes as a quiet assurance, without spectacular displays of God's power. Even Alma, who had been visited by an angel and had seen God sitting on His throne, needed to fast and pray so he could receive a testimony through the power of the Holy Ghost (see Alma 5:45–46; 36:8, 22).

*Your testimony will grow gradually through your experiences.* No one receives a complete testimony all at once. Your testimony will grow stronger through your experiences. It will expand as you show your willingness to serve in the Church, wherever you are called. It will increase as you make decisions to keep the commandments. As you lift and strengthen others, you will see that your testimony continues to develop. As you pray and fast, study the scriptures, attend Church meetings, and hear others share their testimonies, you will be blessed with moments of inspiration that will bolster your testimony. Such moments will come throughout your life as you strive to live the gospel.

*Your testimony will increase as you share it.* Do not wait for your testimony to be fully developed before you share it. Part of a testimony's development comes when it is shared. In fact, you will find that when you give what you have of your testimony, it will be returned to you—with increase.

## Testimony Bearing

In fast and testimony meetings and in conversations you have with family members and friends, you may feel prompted to share your testimony. In such instances, remember that you do not need to share a long, impressive discourse. Your testimony will be most powerful when it is expressed as a brief, heartfelt conviction about the Savior, His teachings, and the Restoration. Pray for guidance, and the Spirit will help you know how to express the feelings in your heart. You will find great joy as you help others share in the hope and assurance the Lord has given you.

Additional references: John 7:17; 1 Corinthians 2:9–14; James 1:5–6; Moroni 10:3–5; D&C 6:22–23; 62:3; 88:81

*See also* Atonement of Jesus Christ; Fasting and Fast Offerings; God the Father; Holy Ghost; Prayer; Revelation; Spiritual Gifts

# Tithing

One of the blessings of membership in The Church of Jesus Christ of Latter-day Saints is the privilege of paying tithing. By living the law of tithing, you participate in building up the kingdom of God on the earth.

Definition and Purpose of Tithing

To pay a full tithe, you give one-tenth of your income to the Lord through His Church. You submit your tithing to a member of your bishopric or branch presidency.

Local leaders transmit tithing funds directly to the headquarters of the Church, where a council determines specific ways to use the sacred funds. This council is comprised of the First Presidency, the Quorum of the Twelve Apostles, and the Presiding Bishopric. Acting according to revelation, they make decisions as they are directed by the Lord. (See D&C 120:1.)

Tithing funds are always used for the Lord's purposes—to build and maintain temples and meetinghouses, to sustain missionary work, and to carry on the work of the Church throughout the world.

Blessings of Paying a Full Tithe

The law of tithing requires sacrifice, but your obedience to the law brings blessings that are far greater than anything you ever give up. The prophet Malachi taught:

"Bring ye all the tithes into the storehouse, that there may be meat in mine house, and prove me now herewith, saith the Lord of hosts, if I will not open you the windows of heaven, and pour you out a blessing, that there shall not be room enough to receive it" (Malachi 3:10).

These blessings come to all who pay a full ten percent of their income, even if that amount is very small. As you obey this law, the Lord will bless you both spiritually and temporally.

Making the Commitment to Pay Tithing

If you have not yet established a pattern of consistent tithe paying, you may have difficulty believing that you can afford to give up one-tenth of your income. But faithful tithe payers learn that they cannot afford *not* to pay tithing. In a very literal and wonderful way, the windows of heaven are opened and blessings are poured out upon them.

Remember that paying tithing is not as much a matter of money as it is a matter of faith. Trust in the Lord. He gave the commandment for our benefit, and He made the accompanying promise. Seek strength in the faith of Nephi, who said, "Let us be faithful in keeping the commandments of the Lord; for behold he is mightier than all the earth" (1 Nephi 4:1).

*See also* Fasting and Fast Offerings

**Tobacco** (*See* Word of Wisdom)

## Unity

Just before the Savior carried out the Atonement, He prayed for His disciples, whom He had sent into the world to teach the gospel. He also prayed for those who would believe in Him because of His disciples' words. He pled for unity: "That they all may be one; as thou, Father, art in me, and I in thee, that they also may be one in us: that the world may believe that thou hast sent me" (John 17:21).

From this prayer we learn how the gospel unites us with Heavenly Father and Jesus Christ and with each other. When we live the gospel, receiving the saving ordinances and keeping our covenants, our natures are changed. The Savior's Atonement sanctifies us, and we can live in unity, enjoying peace in this life and preparing to dwell with the Father and His Son forever.

The Lord has said, "If ye are not one ye are not mine" (D&C 38:27). You can seek and promote this standard of unity in your family and in the Church. If you are married, you and your spouse can be unified in purpose and action. You can allow your unique qualities to complement one another as you face challenges together and grow in love and understanding. You can also be unified with other family members and with members of the Church by serving together, teaching one another, and encouraging one another. You can become one with the President of the Church and other Church leaders as you study their words and follow their counsel.

As the Church grows throughout the world, all Latter-day Saints can be united. Our hearts can be "knit together in unity and in love one towards another" (Mosiah 18:21). We appreciate cultural diversity and individual differences, but we also seek the "unity of the faith" that comes when we follow inspired leaders and remember that we are all children of the same Father (see Ephesians 4:3–6, 11–13).

*See also* Love; Marriage; Obedience; Service; Zion

## **Visiting Teaching** (*See* Relief Society)

## **War**

The Lord has said that in the last days there will be "wars and rumors of wars, and the whole earth shall be in commotion, and men's hearts shall fail them" (D&C 45:26).

As members of The Church of Jesus Christ of Latter-day Saints, we are a people of peace. We follow the Savior, who is the Prince of Peace. We look forward to His millennial reign, when wars will end and peace will be restored to the earth (see Isaiah 2:4). However, we recognize that in this world, government leaders sometimes send military troops to war to defend their nations and ideals.

Latter-day Saints in the military do not need to feel torn between their country and their God. In the Church, "we believe in being subject to kings, presidents, rulers, and magistrates, in obeying, honoring, and sustaining the law" (Articles of Faith 1:12). Military service shows dedication to this principle.

If Latter-day Saints are called upon to go into battle, they can look to the example of Captain Moroni, the great military leader in the Book of Mormon. Although he was a mighty warrior, he "did not delight in bloodshed" (Alma 48:11). He was "firm in the faith of Christ," and his only reason for fighting was to "defend his people, his rights, and his country, and his religion" (Alma 48:13). If Latter-day Saints must go to war, they should go in a spirit of truth and righteousness, with a desire to do good. They should go with love in their hearts for all God's children, including those on the opposing side. Then, if they are required to shed another's blood, their action will not be counted as a sin.

*See also* Civil Government and Law; Peace

**Ward** (*See* Church Administration)

## Welfare

Each member of the Church has two basic welfare responsibilities: to become self-reliant and to care for the poor and the needy.

Parents have a sacred responsibility to look after the physical and spiritual welfare of their children. As children grow older, they become more responsible for their own welfare. Parents should teach them basic principles of welfare, helping them prepare to be self-reliant and provide for their own families in the future. Parents can also give children opportunities to help care for the poor and the needy.

If you are an adult member of the Church, all of the following counsel applies directly to you. If you are a young man or woman, much of this counsel applies to you as well, even if you still depend largely on your parents.

### Becoming Self-Reliant

The responsibility for your social, emotional, spiritual, physical, and economic well-being rests first on yourself, second on your family, and third on the Church. Under the inspiration of the Lord and through your own labors, you should supply yourself and your family with the spiritual and temporal necessities of life.

You are better able to take care of yourself and your family when you are self-reliant. You are prepared to endure times of adversity without becoming dependent on others.

You can become self-reliant by (1) taking advantage of educational opportunities; (2) practicing sound principles of nutrition and hygiene; (3) preparing for and obtaining suitable employment; (4) storing a supply of food and clothing to the extent the law allows; (5) managing your resources wisely, including paying tithes and offerings and avoiding debt; and (6) developing spiritual, emotional, and social strength.

In order to become self-reliant, you must be willing to work. The Lord has commanded us to work (see Genesis 3:19; D&C 42:42). Honorable work is a basic source of happiness, self-worth, and prosperity.

If you are ever temporarily unable to meet your basic needs through your own efforts or the support of family members, the Church may be able to help you. In these situations, the Church often provides life-sustaining resources to help you and your family become self-reliant again.

## Caring for the Poor and the Needy

The Lord has always commanded His people to care for the poor and the needy. He said, "Ye must visit the poor and the needy and administer to their relief" (D&C 44:6). He also commanded, "Remember in all things the poor and the needy, the sick and the afflicted, for he that doeth not these things, the same is not my disciple" (D&C 52:40).

You can care for the poor and the needy in many ways. One important way is through fasting and contributing fast offerings, which the bishop or branch president uses to assist ward or branch members who suffer from poverty, illness, or other hardships. You can also give of your time and share your talents. You can serve the homeless, the disabled, widows, and others in your neighborhood and community.

In addition to giving local and individual care for those in need, the Church reaches out worldwide to people, no matter their faith, who suffer the effects of natural disasters, poverty, disease, and other crises. The Church provides life-sustaining resources to help families and individuals recover and work toward self-reliance. Donations to the Church's Perpetual Education Fund provide the means for disadvantaged Latter-day Saints to further their education. Church-service missionaries volunteer their time and resources to improve literacy, promote health, and provide training.

Additional references: James 1:27; Jacob 2:17–19; D&C 42:31; 104:15–18

*See also* Fasting and Fast Offerings; Service

## Word of Wisdom

The Word of Wisdom is a law of health revealed by the Lord for our physical and spiritual benefit. In this revelation, which is recorded in section 89 of the Doctrine and Covenants, the Lord tells us which foods are good for us to eat and which substances are not good for our bodies. He promises spiritual and physical blessings for obeying the Word of Wisdom.

In the Word of Wisdom, the Lord commands us not to take the following substances into our bodies:

- Alcoholic drinks (see D&C 89:5–7).
- Tobacco (see D&C 89:8).
- Tea and coffee (see D&C 89:9; latter-day prophets have taught that the term "hot drinks" refers to tea and coffee).

Anything harmful that people purposefully take into their bodies is not in harmony with the Word of Wisdom. This is especially true of illegal drugs, which can destroy those who become addicted to them. Stay entirely away from them. Do not experiment with them. The abuse of prescription drugs also leads to destructive addiction.

The Lord declares that the following foods are good for our bodies:

- Vegetables and fruits, which should be used "with prudence and thanksgiving" (see D&C 89:10–11).
- The flesh "of beasts and of the fowls of the air," which is "to be used sparingly" (see D&C 89:12–13).
- Grains such as wheat, rice, and oats, which are "the staff of life" (see D&C 89:14–17).

Blessings from Keeping the Word of Wisdom

To those who keep the Word of Wisdom, the Lord promises:

"All saints who remember to keep and do these sayings, walking in obedience to the commandments, shall receive health in their navel and marrow to their bones;

"And shall find wisdom and great treasures of knowledge, even hidden treasures;

"And shall run and not be weary, and shall walk and not faint.

"And I, the Lord, give unto them a promise, that the destroying angel shall pass by them, as the children of Israel, and not slay them" (D&C 89:18–21).

Overcoming Addiction

The best course is to completely avoid the substances that the Lord prohibits in the Word of Wisdom. But if you have become addicted to any of these substances, you can become free from your addiction. You can overcome addiction through personal effort, the enabling power of the Lord's grace, help from family members and friends, and guidance from Church leaders.

Pray for help, and do all in your power to resist temptations that come because of addiction. Your Heavenly Father wants you to receive the blessings that come from keeping the

Word of Wisdom, and He will strengthen you in your sincere efforts to do so.

Additional references: D&C 49:19–21; 59:15–20; 88:124; 89:1–4

*See also* Obedience; Temptation

## Worship

To worship God is to give Him your love, reverence, service, and devotion. The Lord commanded Moses, "Worship God, for him only shalt thou serve" (Moses 1:15). In this dispensation He has commanded, "Thou shalt love the Lord thy God with all thy heart, with all thy might, mind, and strength; and in the name of Jesus Christ thou shalt serve him" (D&C 59:5). If you place any person or thing above the love of God, you are practicing false worship, or idolatry (see Exodus 20:3–6).

Prayer is one way you can worship the Father. Alma taught his son Helaman, "Cry unto God for all thy support; yea, let all thy doings be unto the Lord, and whithersoever thou goest let it be in the Lord; yea, let all thy thoughts be directed unto the Lord; yea, let the affections of thy heart be placed upon the Lord forever" (Alma 37:36).

You should attend your Church meetings in a spirit of worship. The Lord has commanded: "That thou mayest more fully keep thyself unspotted from the world, thou shalt go to the house of prayer and offer up thy sacraments upon my holy day; for verily this is a day appointed unto you to rest from your labors, and to pay thy devotions unto the Most High" (D&C 59:9–10).

Participation in priesthood ordinances is also part of your worship. As you reverently partake of the sacrament and attend the temple, you remember and worship your Heavenly Father and express your gratitude for His Son, Jesus Christ.

In addition to showing outward expressions of worship, you should have a worshipful attitude wherever you go and in everything you do. Alma taught this principle to a group of people who had been cast out of their place of worship. He helped them see that true worship is not limited to one day of the week (see Alma 32:11). Speaking to the same group of people, Alma's companion Amulek encouraged them to "worship God, in whatsoever place ye may be in, in spirit and in truth" (Alma 34:38).

Additional references: Psalm 95:6–7; Mosiah 18:25; Alma 33:2–11; D&C 20:17–19, 29; Articles of Faith 1:11

*See also* Fasting and Fast Offerings; God the Father; Love; Prayer; Sabbath

## Zion

The Doctrine and Covenants contains many passages in which the Lord commands the Saints to "seek to bring forth and establish the cause of Zion" (D&C 6:6; see also D&C 11:6; 12:6; 14:6).

The word *Zion* has various meanings in the scriptures. The most general definition of the word is "the pure in heart" (D&C 97:21). *Zion* is often used in this way to refer to the Lord's people or to the Church and its stakes (see D&C 82:14).

In the early days of this dispensation, Church leaders counseled members to build up Zion by emigrating to a central location. Today our leaders counsel us to build up Zion wherever we live. Members of the Church are asked to remain in their native lands and help establish the Church there. Many temples are being built so that Latter-day Saints throughout the world can receive temple blessings.

The word *Zion* can also refer to specific geographic locations, as follows:

- The city of Enoch (see Moses 7:18–21).
- The ancient city of Jerusalem (see 2 Samuel 5:6–7; 1 Kings 8:1; 2 Kings 9:28).

- The New Jerusalem, which will be built in Jackson County, Missouri (see D&C 45:66–67; 57:1–3; Articles of Faith 1:10).

Additional references: Isaiah 2:2–3; 1 Nephi 13:37; D&C 35:24; 39:13; 45:68–71; 59:3–4; 64:41–43; 90:36–37; 97:18–28; 101:16–18; 105:5; 115:5–6; 136:31